SCANDINAVIA
LIVING DESIGN

ELIZABETH GAYNOR • PHOTOGRAPHS BY KARI HAAVISTO

STEWART, TABORI & CHANG
NEW YORK

To Vepsi

Originally published in hardcover
by Stewart, Tabori & Chang in 1987.

Paperback edition published in 1994
and distributed in the U.S.
by Stewart, Tabori & Chang, Inc.
575 Broadway, New York, NY 10012.

Distributed in the English language
elsewhere in the world (except Canada and
Central and South America) by Melia
Publishing Services, P.O. Box 1639,
Maidenhead, Berkshire SL6 6YZ England.
Canadian and Central and South American
accounts should contact Sales Manager,
Stewart, Tabori & Chang.

**Library of Congress Cataloging-in-
Publication Data**

Gaynor, Elizabeth, 1946–
  Scandinavia, living design.

  Bibliography: p.
  1. Architecture, Domestic—
Scandinavia.   2. Vernacular
architecture—Scandinavia.   3. Interior
architecture—Scandinavia.   4. Interior
decoration—Scandinavia.   I. Title.
NA7370.G39 1987   728′.0948   87-9966
ISBN 1-55670-009-1 (hardcover)
ISBN 1-55670-364-3 (paperback)

Printed in Japan

10 9 8 7 6 5 4 3 2 1

PAGE 1: *Finnish designer Simo Heikkilä's
Experimental Chair, originally made in 1982 to
test ergonomics and now available in limited
edition.* PAGES 2–3: *the graphic painted interior
of an eighteenth-century Norwegian timber
house from the Hemesdal valley.* PAGE 4: *on the
coast of Denmark, an early twentieth-century
octagonal cottage in the neoclassical style.* PAGE
5: *textile and kitchen tools hang in a Swedish
kitchen.*

OPPOSITE: *romantic rural church architecture in Finland.* OVERLEAF: *summer garden
flowers in a log house.*

CONTENTS

INTRODUCTION

The countries of Scandinavia—Denmark, Finland, Norway, Sweden, and Iceland—lie in the most northerly corner of Europe. Historically, this location—with four of the five physically separated from the European mainland and with a substantial area of three of them lying above the Arctic Circle—has preserved both their isolation and their cultural integrity. Even Denmark, whose islands and Jutland peninsula serve as a kind of bridge from the Scandinavian peninsula to the Continent, shares with her sister countries of Norway, Sweden, and Finland an orientation toward the Baltic Sea that drew her to them in matters of living and language. The hardship and deprivation imposed by rigors of climate and geography characterized life in much of Sweden, Finland, Norway, Iceland, and parts of Denmark and not only allied these countries in cultural and commercial sympathy, but fostered among their residents a set of altruistic ways that has had lasting social consequences.

Perhaps no other body of nations so eloquently and dramatically illustrates what author Lawrence Durrell refers to as "spirit of place"—that is, the expression of a locale as much through its wildflowers and weather as through its inhabitants and their customs, which have been molded by the environment. Scandinavia's landscape has shaped its people and how they live. No-choice climatic circumstances have always ordered the region's priorities; physical demands have molded its values. Tangible expressions of geographical determinism abound in the everyday life of Scandinavia, and in the realm of living design in particular. Tradition stands for methods that work and results that last, whether in making a useful object or in building a house. In lands with relatively few resources, simple solutions proved best. The tradition of simplicity remains unrivaled in these countries, which remained agrarian until this century; love of handwork still characterizes their sparse populations, whose ancestors learned to rely on their own skills to survive. Even when waves of Continental influence have affected the region's taste, Scandinavians applied characteristic restraint and preference for the plain to rework lines to fit their simple, rustic-derived dwellings. More than any one recognizable style, Scandinavian living design represents a way of life, a manner of setting up home with certain features common to all five countries; the stylistic distinctions that do exist are more likely to be a function of geographical specifics than of political boundary. This book is an attempt to place the residential architecture, home objects, and fine crafts from this part of the world into a context of social culture and to demonstrate the crucial role that nature has always played in shaping lifestyles.

"Others imagine that Scandinavia is a place where one sits and gnaws his fingernails and where paranoia and perversion flourish during the long winter months," said Alf Bøe, curator of the Munch Museum in Oslo. Indeed, the remoteness of the Nordic countries has bred misperceptions nearly as colorful as the mythic tales recorded in their rich ancient sagas. The winter season, when the sun does not shine for weeks at a time in the northernmost areas, is countered by a summer unequaled for its lush greenery and intense light. Coping with winter fosters ingenuity; the unspoiled summer environment is a seasonal reward. True, the stillness of the gray, cold period has exacted a toll in seriousness and introspection that also manifests itself in planning and design, but a jubilant sense of humanity and break-free exuberance reflect the warm flip side of life in these homogeneous societies, in which everyone can count on physical well-being and enjoyment of nature's bounty. Habit and law set high standards among Scandinavian citizens for living conditions, occupational opportunities, and play. Countries thrust into the buffer zone between hostile superpowers in the twentieth century have, by virtue of necessity, largely withdrawn from the fray. Their attention and resources can be directed toward that elusive goal, quality of life, and toward the development of living solutions that benefit the whole society. Quietly and with determination, many such aims have been approached if not totally achieved. Long life expectancy, high literacy, the world's lowest infant-mortality rates, and freedom from poverty generally characterize Nordic life.

Here are old societies but young republics who seem to enjoy the benefits of both. Political interconnections have shaped their allegiances and dependencies on one another, making of the five a family of nations with little residual antipathy, with few formal alliances but many similar states of mind. Background data have the ring of a riddle: Norway, during her history, has been governed by both Denmark and Sweden, Finland by both Sweden and tsarist Russia, Iceland by Denmark and Norway, and part of Sweden by Denmark. Sweden and Denmark, great royal realms in their day, now coexist as equals with their neighbors. In all five countries, old-world civility and new-world industry now peacefully commingle. Social progressiveness breathes life into well-entrenched traditional values. Like other European countries, the five live with a deep respect for custom but, like America, vigorously pursue a better future. Like Americans, Scandinavians are rugged frontiersmen who know the value of hard work; but like Continental Europeans, they refuse to discard the past for the potential of the present. These are lands of castles and cabins, both beautiful and sophisticated in their simplicity, and each is appreciated for its contribution to the texture of life.

Scandinavians are people who venerate good architecture, but not at the expense of the natural environment. Their designs have won prizes in world competitions and figure in important collections of international museums, yet understatement and usefulness blend them into the high general level of production at home rather than bequeath them superstar status.

Scandinavian design and architecture came into their own in the modern era. Feeling the effects of the Industrial Revolution nearly a century after southern Europe and the United States, the Nordic countries learned from the failings of other nations and set up systems to ensure the welfare of a displaced rural population called to urban jobs and settlement. Many of the Scandinavian nations were not only able to ward off the potential miseries of slum housing and pollution, but also applied modern solutions to their great growth spurts, which had the effect of socializing and politicizing design. Architecture and design, in modern times as before, were to be geared to man and his place in nature. Products reflected values: objects must relate to human proportions and comfort (ergonomics), needs (functionalism), and spirit (beauty). And modern pieces found their place alongside objects and structures from other eras. These values and aesthetics had always been linked, promoting a rather easy marriage between crafts and industrial design, between vernacular buildings and new architecture. Today the intention is to funnel resources toward the general good rather than into runaway consumer markets. Conveying the ethics perceived as inherent in industrial production and architecture, Danish author Villy Sørensen once said, "Getting more of something is good—but getting something good is better."

Luxury knows bounds in Scandinavia. One consequence is that the region produces some of the world's first-rate everyday objects. A dominant approach is to steer clear of reinventing the wheel, focusing instead on the refinement of ideas that work and on the satisfaction of real needs. Sectors forgotten in other societies receive serious attention; quality goods and housing are created for the young, elderly, and disabled. Great strides have been made in energy-conscious construction, solidly based on passive solutions learned over centuries of dealing with the cold. Scandinavians have applied to modern production their rural fingertip-feeling for wood. Factory-made furniture and accessories still show evidence of handwork and careful detailing, and this sensitivity toward materials has been transferred to glass, steel, and plastics.

Through pictures of houses and background text, this book attempts to give a domestic framework to lifestyles in Iceland, Norway, Sweden, Finland, and Denmark. Dwellings are grouped not by country, but by their locations in landscapes that have had everything to do with how they became what they are. Architects and designers are covered insofar as their work is represented in the featured homes. Indeed, most places are owner-designed, reflecting the hands-on attitude of people to whom the importance of shelter is mirrored in their deep love of home. Well-known names like Poul Kjaerholm, Bruno Mathsson, Arne Jacobsen, Alvar Aalto, and many contemporary designers/architects are mentioned in passing or not at all owing more to the availability of homes for photography, and the limitations of time and distance, than to any judgment on the worthiness of their work. But an effort has been made to document houses and apartments of representative styles from all five countries and different periods. This is a volume on interior design as well as residential architecture, precluding the coverage of some houses of architectural merit whose furnishings did not lend themselves to photography. It does not focus specifically on the design objects and crafts for which Scandinavia is so well known, as these subjects have been scrupulously covered in other books. Regrettably, some of the newest design is not included, as so much has not yet been absorbed into picture-ready homes; our travels limited us to what we found in place.

This book does not argue for or against differences in living styles from one country to another, but acknowledges the commonalities of life in the extreme north. It is hoped that the photographs of houses in their locales will allow the reader to draw his own conclusions on these issues. Design that specifically addresses social problems is not shown here—for example, the planning and products for special groups like the elderly and the disabled, where the Scandinavians have met with much success. And no effort has been made to explore the living situations of minorities like the indigenous Samis (Lapps) or scattered northern farmers or to give a true picture of life in a typical or planned Nordic town. Such matters are beyond the scope of this work. Instead, this is a look at some of the loveliest of Scandinavian homes, at beautiful solutions for living, cooking, play, and sometimes work. Some are grand, some are modest, but all share in the spirit of fundamental connection to a distinctive land. Most are not showy in luxurious terms, but their validity and staying power are as certain as that of the earliest settlers in the toughest terrain. The reserved good looks of these houses reflect the temperament of their owners who, like most Scandinavians, seem to believe a good secret is best kept quiet.

C H A P T E R O N E

FROM THE FOREST

If Scandinavia is regarded as the last wilderness of Europe, then her great northern forests have, to a certain extent, earned her that status. Even today, these dark, silent expanses stretch across the surfaces of Finland, Sweden, and Norway, standing, as they always have, between clusters of people living on land claimed from roots that grew slowly and ran deep. Forested land supplied simple foods like game, berries, and mushrooms; yielded wood for the superior sailing vessels of the Viking era; provided the chief source of fuel, building materials, and preservatives. Forests also represented the first impediment to overcome before man could get to the business of cultivating crops, tending livestock, and plying abundant waters for fish. Forests still play a dual role—as a replenishable resource to a world hungry for wood and paper products and also as a barrier between the people whose relative isolation has shaped the ways they think and live.

Finland's vast forests, which still cover two-thirds of that country, and Norway's unique blend of mountains and woods historically qualified these countries as the peripheries of the periphery. Lack of other resources kept both in the shade longer than their former rulers, Sweden and Denmark. Only Iceland, 600 miles out to sea, was farther adrift from the currents of change. Sweden, which extends nearly 1,000 miles from polar tip to arable toe, had a greater range of resources and offered more potential for their development. And Denmark, a low land whose soil was suited to farming, tamed her majestic beech forests so that they eventually became sources of pleasure and privacy more often than produce. Iceland is said to have had trees when Norwegians first landed there in the late ninth century, but man's enthusiasm in clearing them for pasture and putting the wood to practical use stripped her of this resource. Nature's quixotic temperament has kept her nearly barren of wood.

The dark of winter brought man indoors. Snug cabins of squared, hand-hewn logs with dovetail joints were built spacious enough to accommodate woodworking, which was practiced by fireside and in the glow of wood tapers. Within the main room cooking vessels and tools, beds and cupboards, sleds and hunting gear were all fashioned of wood with a sureness of hand passed from father to son in extended-family homesteads. Cut juniper and pine branches sometimes freshened wide plank floors around central hearths in outposts where rugs were a luxury. Practical home-crafted solutions to problems of furnishing resulted in simple shapes and sturdy built-in pieces. While in Finland and northern Sweden strict proportion and line brought plain harmony to most home objects, Norwegians drew on the ornamental proficiency of their Viking past to carve and vividly paint intricate motifs in trims and moldings. Self-reliance in home skills was taught by solitude. As the descendants of northern Norwegian woodsmen still say, "Any man who can't do everything is an idiot." Such attitudes toward the crafting of home objects paved the way for contemporary achievements in wood and other natural materials.

What one generation started, the next would finish. Young families inherited the main cabin as their parents aged and accommodated the older couple in an adjoining structure, freely adding to the courtyardlike complex of wood buildings comprising their home. The groundwork in interior furnishings having been laid by their elders, a young man and wife might venture at decorating further with paint and textiles. The threat of fire was one consideration in such multibuilding arrangements; saunas in Finland were almost always separate structures, as were cooking sheds that were used in warmer weather. Other outbuildings housed animals, fodder, extra clothing, tools, and supplies. These unheated storage structures were converted to summer sleeping quarters for hired hands, if the family was prosperous enough to have them, and for unmarried children of courting age, whose availability to suitors was unabashedly ensured during the romantic, light summer nights.

Centuries of practice taught the Nordics about the responsiveness of well-handled natural materials to the extremes of their climate, and the experience has served them well in modern fuel-dependent times. The heavy log walls of forest cabins provided insulation from winter's cold, evenly radiating daytime heat back at night. Careful notching kept walls free from drafts; bits of moss or turf were used to plug worn spaces. Massive fireplaces of stone, with surfaces later covered by stucco, were stoked all day long for cooking and heating; their surfaces and long flues retained warmth long after embers died. Window openings were oriented to the south and kept minimal, their frames fitted tight against winter's icy drafts. Steeply pitched roofs with generous overhangs insured against the weight of heavy snows. Birch bark laid out in flat pieces was covered by split poles or turf that grew thick with the passing years, all the better to insulate the house from the seasonal chill.

Primeval forests gave rise to tales to explain nature's mysteries. The inky darkness of the months-long winter night kept the deep woods in constant shadow, erratically illuminated by eerie waves of northern lights reflected against the constant snow cover. Alone in the forest or at home, the mind was free to wander, to see spirits in gnarled trees and sense the supernatural in dim surroundings. Pagan epics were passed along by recitation, a legacy of heroic history left to modern man when these narratives were written down in later years. Forests were to Norsemen what the proverbial briar patch was to Br'er Rabbit—that familiar habitat imprinted upon the soul since birth. The woods have remained a welcoming sanctuary into which one can slip unnoticed—on cross-country skis or with mushroom-gathering basket in hand—or in which to build a house without disturbing the all-embracing evergreen cover.

PRECEDING PAGES: *a modern version of the old Finnish box chair,* PAGE 13, *one of the earliest pieces of furniture found in the primitive chimneyless hut; such a seat was used for storage and as a place of honor for the master of the house. Winter paints a black-and-white landscape of a forest's evergreens and birches,* PAGES 14–15.

CLOCKWISE, FROM ABOVE: *the marvelously intricate carving on a Norwegian stave church from the thirteenth century. Brushes and brooms are made from tree roots. Log rafts are guided through a canal linking rivers and lakes, the watery highways for trees harvested in northern Scandinavia. In wooded country areas of Finland, a scooter-type sled provides transportation for people of all ages. Wild blueberries and chanterelles picked from the forest floor are sold in open markets.*

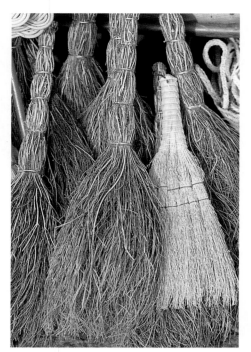

As in Childhood

I am like many city people. We all dream of our childhoods in the country where we grew our own potatoes and bathed in our own saunas. For me, this place is everything I had as a child," says Kirsti Rantanen of the log house in Finland, just an hour from Helsinki, where she now makes her home. A full-income, five-year government grant, much sought after by the artistic community, was awarded her several years ago for her textile work. It allows her the freedom of a sabbatical from university teaching, as well as year-round country living with her retired husband.

Bought for weekend stays around twenty-five years ago, a small cottage (without electricity or water) and its several outbuildings served the Rantanen family as a country getaway from June until September every year and for such holidays as Easter, Midsummer, and Christmas. Candlelit days and nights made the cottage a romantic winter retreat; the coming of spring was announced by the shift of shadows. In the early 1970s, the cottage was converted to a textile studio and a barn was resituated, creating a traditional open courtyard set-up, and a larger main house was moved here from Finland's west coast. Like other timber structures no longer in use, this "new" log house was purchased, marked log by log and transported, then reassembled in a few weeks' time. Insulation was added on the outside, leaving interior log walls exposed, and a new board-and-battan exterior was repainted in its original, typically western colors. The two-tone combination visually cuts the height of the house, bringing it into line with the other single-story red wood structures on the property. Its new location sets the main house on the highest spot on the wooded site, with a view to a nearby lake.

With a bit of artistic license, Mrs. Rantanen has succeeded in re-creating the feeling of a traditional Finnish *tupa*, or one-room cabin, in the main room. The century-old farmhouse had sheltered three generations in its original locale, the farmer and his wife sleeping in the built-in bed in the main room, their parents in one adjoining room, and a son and his wife in the other. The unheated second floor was used only for summer sleeping. Now the main room serves generally for sitting and dining, but overnight guests are still accommodated on a period trundle bed. The large corner stove dominates the space, as it always has, from what was once called the "women's corner" in the warmest part of the house, where cooking, sewing and other crafts were practiced. This is a room that changes with the seasons; the textiles are rotated with the calendar celebrations, much as they might have been in an old Finnish log home. In its warm-weather dress donned for Midsummer, seen here, blues and whites provide a background for a bouquet of shades taken from summer flowers. The furnishings and favorite objects are mixed in an uncontrived arrangement. Some belonged to the farmer who originally owned the house, some are from the early days of the Rantanens' marriage, others are from friends. Says Mrs. Rantanen, "It's just a collection of small details."

The sauna, ABOVE, *was on the property. It stands a walk away from the wooded lake for secluded after-bath plunges. Icons and old-style tapers,* OPPOSITE, *recall Mrs. Rantanen's childhood in Karelia, Finland's Orthodox easternmost province, which was lost to Russia after World War II. Typically, the golden images glowed in a corner cabinet, illuminated by candles, where a visitor would pause for a moment of religious respect before greeting his host. Here, a more playful group of objects lighten the meaning.*

In the traditional set-up, a long pine table pulls up to a built-in bench, OPPOSITE. Overhead poles where textiles are now draped were originally for hanging bread that was baked in great batches and made with holes in the centers. Woven birch-bark baskets are for serving it. LEFT: warm afternoon sun lights the wooden, two-tone main house and the cottage/studio. ABOVE: Mrs. Rantanen's wild raspberry-and-blueberry tart and an antique Karelian ceramic bowl.

Baking-paper cutouts decorate shelf edges in a china cupboard, ABOVE. The farmhouse's well-worn front door, BELOW. An early nineteenth-century trundle bed is decked out with textiles, RIGHT. A farm-style Biedermeier chair stands by curtains that are simply suspended from string, as in the old days.

The strong lines of the main room, ABOVE, are reinforced by long rag runners designed by Kirsti Rantanen and made by a local farmer's wife. Textile collections warm the log room and reflect the weaver-owner's interests. Traditional Finnish embroidered linens, RIGHT. A collector's kitchen window, OPPOSITE.

In the Timber Tradition

In a clearing surrounded by a birch and spruce forest stands a house built six years ago in the Norwegian timber tradition. Family property, situated just far enough north of Oslo to seclude it safely from urban encroachment, came into the hands of the present owner. In the ashes of the main house that had once stood on the spot before catching fire, a new structure was erected, borrowing from peasant architectural detailing. This romantic approach to the construction of a new home mimics to some extent the spirit of the latter half of the nineteenth century, when Norway, like some of the other Scandinavian countries, fell in love with the past en route to finding its own way into the modern era. At a time when Rousseau concocted jungles of exaggerated house plants to add a primitive atmosphere to his oils and Gauguin went to Tahiti in search of the untainted, Norwegians dipped into the unique blend of rustic and Viking expressions that characterized their "native" craft. The so-called Swiss look, fascinated with roof forms, verandas, and wooden projections, represented a step in the evolution of romantic timber fashions that culminated in the full-blown "dragon style," which employed ani-

mistic motifs and rich carvings based on the Viking heritage.

The romantic attitude of this structure seems well suited to the collection of Norwegian folk antiques purchased to furnish the interior. Wooden pieces, either finished naturally or painted, endow the contemporary home with the flavor of the past and the appeal of the handmade. Furnishings of the seventeenth through nineteenth centuries from various parts of the country are combined with more regard for scale and surface than for period. The success of the mostly rural mix depends on the generous interior spaces clad in plain pine paneling, which provides a warm, woodsy background ample enough to continue to absorb bits of Norway's colorful history.

The old forested property on which the new house is situated includes some vintage outbuildings like the stabur, *or storehouse,* LEFT. *A pilasterlike motif on the main house,* BELOW, *can be seen to have been taken from the* stabur'*s detailing. Old wooden skis fit over boots by means of simple leather thongs.* OPPOSITE: *looking out from one terrace past two balconied verandas toward the trees, feathery-frosty with new snow and ice on an all-white winter day.*

PRECEDING PAGES: *a grouping of carved folk objects on shelves that form part of a bed-surround include food vessels, a nineteenth-century clock, and a pair of decorative V-shaped yokes for draft horses, with exceptional figurative and geometric motifs.*

A painted bed and connected cabinets, ABOVE, *taken from an early nineteenth-century log dwelling in eastern Norway, has been filled with pillows and weavings for living-room lounging or putting up a guest for the night. Carved animal containers parade across the mantel of a stucco fireplace,* LEFT; *the lion is a nineteenth-century tobacco box.*

In the dining area, ABOVE, high-back Baroque-style chairs stand near a country table, painted armoire, and nineteenth-century oils. Paneling covers the log construction of the house inside and out, except for substantial support beams left exposed in the living room ceiling, RIGHT. An unmatched peasant wall cabinet and table make a setting for found panels, beer tankards, and an intricately carved food box.

OUT OF THE SHADOW

"Here, you are either an admirer or detractor of Aalto," says architect Markus Aaltonen, alluding to the plight of many Finnish architects working in Alvar Aalto's shadow. In his homeland, the influence of this architectural heavyweight is almost a given. Not only do his prominent works mark the urban landscape of Helsinki and large and small towns throughout the country, but Aalto's distinctive furniture designs are enjoying a revival, both inside and outside Finland, that, twenty years after his death, is popularizing them beyond any expectations.

Markus Aaltonen graduated from the architectural university at Otaniemi, whose campus itself was designed by Aalto. Rather than dodge the issue, as some of his contemporaries do, Aaltonen freely acknowledges a professional debt to the master. In this house, his first full residential project, he more than satisfies that debt by finding his own vigorous expression for what has been passed on.

Working in tandem with his wife, an interior architect, he designed for their clients a house that is wedded through line and orientation to the surrounding pine forest and rocky landscape. The white-clean-through structure of mortar-washed brick

and wood has an inside/outside integrity, owing to the visual accessibility of its forms from many points. By turning its undulating two-story wall with window bays and decks toward the view over treetops from the granite slope, Aaltonen presents its owners with a soaring view that sets them within, yet above, the dusky woods. Free experimentation with window rhythms and placement capitalizes on the private setting and pulls light through openings to the back of the interior. Surface play and varied materials both outside and in throw the monochrome scheme into relief. Costs were kept reasonable through limiting the range of building elements and by engaging the granite outcropping to support the structure. The idea is an old one in Finland. Says the architect, "I simply put stone on stone."

OPPOSITE: *the crisp white structure pierced by windows of varying dimensions faces a secluded forest. The undulation of the central portion cuts the inner corner on the right-angled form. A central staircase is pivotal in the open main-floor plan,* LEFT. *Pine floors were stained translucent granite-gray throughout. Heat is radiated down from panels mounted behind the ceiling; it passes through the air and seeks warm solid masses.*

Four fireplaces, including one that fuels the sauna, feed into a core flue. In the living room, TOP, *built-in banquettes are partly covered by a cascading weaving by Maija Lavonen. A second-floor balcony is flooded with sun above the treetops,* ABOVE. *Cotton printed textiles here and elsewhere are by Marimekko. On the lowest level, a swimming pool for after-sauna plunges had to be blasted out of the bedrock,* LEFT.

LIFE IMITATES ART

In Hertha Hillfon's studio home, designed by her architect-husband, Gosta, there is a seamless continuum between illusion and reality. Few guideposts indicate where art leaves off and life begins; no physical barriers separate the symbolic from the functional. Mrs. Hillfon's ceramic pieces, like her environment, tend to romanticize the everyday, to cast the commonplace in a different light. A homemade grain bread becomes an art object and takes its place in a kitchen still life; a large-as-life chair sculpture also serves simply as a place to sit. Just beyond the door, a colossal ceramic foot protrudes from beneath some leaves; smooth clay faces wait in silence behind a veil of deep green vines.

Gosta Hillfon's work designing archaeological exhibits—such as for ancient gravesites in the Egyptian desert—would seem to qualify him to create the right sort of building to house his wife's ceramic play of the inanimate against the living. Tucked in a small wood near Stockholm, behind the house in which he grew up, is the rectangular studio where she works and where they both like to spend a good deal of their time. The simple volume is sheltered from the old house by pleasantly overgrown shrubs. Out back, an herb garden plays hopscotch with the large limestone squares that, with overhead trellis, form a modest loggia. Inside, light-filled rooms give onto one another without doors, with the expansive studio as the core space. Native materials form the architecturally textured backdrop for an amalgam of new and old furnishings and timeless art.

Surface and scale are the two chief determinants of the effective blend. A rough plaster wall is a foil for a precise wood staircase that visually floats between the center hall and upstairs library. An unfinished wood frame above a bed is draped with woolly blankets and weavings, making a cozy, behind-the-stove "sleeping shelf" that hangs suspended above the smooth limestone floor. Large works in ceramic, placed in generously proportioned rooms, make a heroic world of their mundane subjects. There is a grace about these pieces, nothing overstated or coarse in their sliding scale of expression. The smoothing touch of hands that are equally at home with homespun textiles, the slow turn of a grain mill, and massive chunks of clay assures that details are refined. A capable artist whose work embodies the strength of custom in women's craft, Mrs. Hillfon freely admires her husband's ability to give form to her need for creative space: "He is the man who holds up the roof."

An exterior view of the studio shows the large half-round window that breaks the flatness of its surface, LEFT. *A life-size ceramic chair adds an artful touch to the kitchen/dining space,* OPPOSITE. *The sheet-metal oven surround and hood were designed by Mr. Hillfon to complement the sensuous shapes of his wife's work.*

OVERLEAF: *an artful, altarlike arrangement of objects makes sacred the profane. Strong ceramic shapes sculpted by Mrs. Hillfon— a "melting" flat bread, ladle, jug, and large water vessel—are set off by dried grasses, a hank of flax, and fresh garden blossoms.*

The edges of a dove cage in a hallway are softened with hung textiles and a sheaf of wheat, ABOVE. A discontinuous ceiling and clean-crafted, open stairway define the uncomplicated hall and frame a ceramic cupboard by the artist, RIGHT.

A summer meal under the trees has the allure of a moment in a capsule, a still life set with heavy bleached linens, smoked fish, and tabletop accessories that do not match.

A spot for musing or taking an afternoon nap is tucked into a corner behind the kitchen, ABOVE. Mrs. Hillfon's meditative ceramic faces in the leaves, RIGHT.

THE NOBILITY OF THE RUSTIC

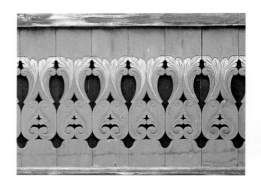

I n the land of the trolls and ancient Norwegian sagas stands an unusual timber farmstead poised high on a hill, asserting its presence to the valley below. This dark relic, with its dominant clock-tower and ample log structures, stands at an old royal station that was used at least as far back as the ninth century. It was here that kings and their retinues changed horses and rested on long journeys northward from the Oslo Fjord, for this is the valley of Gudbrandsdalen, the major artery through a mountainous, wooded country where few routes were direct and none were easy. It is said that the King of the Trolls, the Giant of the surrounding Dovre Mountains, stood by the side of King Harald Haarfager (or Fairhair) when he fought the battles that first united Norway 1,000 years ago.

The family at Tofte—the farm bears their name—claim Harald as their ancestor. As then, they work the land, proud of their long attachment to the soil and role in history as local stationmasters. The story is told that when Prince Christian Fredrik of Denmark stopped here in the sixteenth century, his farmer-host remarked, "The prince and I have royal blood and we must talk alone," leading the visitor behind closed doors for a private schnapps.

Such a rustic estate is rare today; parts of it are several centuries old. A traveler's log from the mid-nineteenth century describes the main room and gives details that document the self-sufficiency of life at an isolated farm: "There were the winter coats, the bear skins and furs, and reindeer boots and high waterboots; the blankets and comfortables and dresses; then the little sleds and sleighs for the snow; the piles of round oatmeal cakes, each a foot and a half in diameter, kept for the food of the laborers; heaps of birch bark for tanning, spinning-wheels for weaving, shoe-blocks for shoe-making—for on these farms all trades are carried on."

Some of the exterior woodwork, FAR LEFT, shows intricate carving, a Viking skill handed down through the centuries, and the rare blend of gilt work on deep-stained timber. Four of the buildings, loosely grouped around the courtyard, LEFT. A detail of the timber and stone dairy barn, BOTTOM LEFT, and its painted lintel. OPPOSITE: the grand armoire, ABOVE, boasts regal gilt carvings and naïvely painted panels depicting mythical figures in the actual farm settings. It was uncommon for such a piece to be built around a window. Items in the early nineteenth-century dowry chest, BELOW: a traditional crown worn by the bride during the marriage ceremony and a trio of embroidered waist purses.

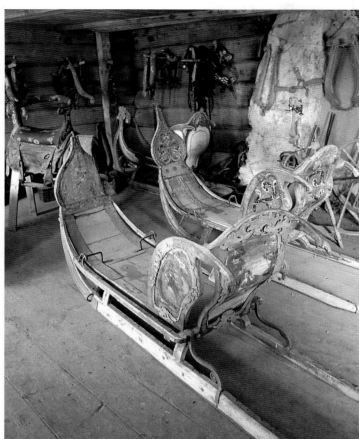

A detail of the armoire and painted wall border shows an elegance that befits kingly visits but is otherwise unexpected in a remote farm's "best room," LEFT. Sleds that carried kings and their ladies show beautiful painted work, ABOVE.

COLLECTOR'S CHOICE

Salmon fishing with his father in the river valleys of Norway cultivated in Preben Mehren not only a taste for fresh seafood but also for the treasures of his country's rural past. Following his father's lead, he succumbed to the purchase of his first rustic antique at the age of thirteen, and by his early manhood he had acquired an entire cabin with its interior fittings intact.

In a country like Norway, where particular pockets of culture are kept alive by a mountainous terrain that defies easy passage, the past is only as far as some of the remote river valleys. Mehren has culled from that past some outstanding examples of rural craftsmanship and reassembled them in the homestead he devised with his accumulated finds. Two whole log dwellings, a balconied *stabur* (storage barn), a stable, and turf-roofed doghouse are among the structures he has grouped on a mountainside site overlooking Oslo Fjord.

The two log houses, used mostly for entertaining and for accommodating guests —there is also a contemporary home built for the family—are remarkable not only for their architecture but for their interior design, which conveys the spirit of the valley from which each comes. The slate-roofed cabin from Gudbrandsdalen, in central Norway, is exceptional for its delicately painted doors with naïve tree motifs and the intricate, lacy woodwork of certain furnishings. The spacious main room was conceived for all functions. A table that now easily seats thirty served for work and preparing food as well as for dining. Ingenious economy of line accounts for nearly all needs in cleverly built-in fittings, while more extravagant

carving and painted effects color the whole and attest to the skills of its former inhabitants.

The house from the Hemsedal valley, built in the eighteenth century, as the other one was, has an interior remarkable for the decorative effects on all the wood surfaces. These were accomplished in 1850 by the most celebrated "rose-painter" in the country, Tomas Luraas. (Rose-painting, the art of embellishing wood with motifs inspired by field and garden, is unique to Norway.) This exceptional fellow was an itinerant craftsman from the province of Telemark. He perfected his skills partly as a way to stay several steps ahead of the authorities, by whom he was wanted for his equally dexterous counterfeiting of currency. Luraas moved from valley to valley, offering to decorate ceilings, walls, and furniture for families in return for a place to hide. Virtually every surface of the main room bears his artistry, restored here and there after the house was moved.

The slate chimney and turf roof of the cabin from the Hemsedal valley and a detail of the stabur, *showing its silvery weathered front and heavy, turned-log corner posts,* ABOVE.

On a cleared mountainside site, log buildings from Norway's valleys surround the chaletlike main house, built in 1971, ABOVE. Several of the structures, including the doghouse, RIGHT, have turf roofs. An underlay of birch bark curls out from the grassy cover.

OVERLEAF: in the Gudbrandsdalen house, the main room's built-in cupboard has elaborately carved crown molding and brackets, characteristic of the valley (PAGE 50). A sun-streaked line-up of country chairs around the long pine table, TOP RIGHT. Painted doors with a well-worn naïve tree motif lead to entry hall and bedroom (PAGE 51). The empty clock case has been refitted for hanging linens.

The Hemsedal house has an unusual loft arrangement, reached by ladder, with beds tucked under the angle of the roof. Rose-painting covers every beam, molding, cupboard, door, and even the clock, OPPOSITE. The timepiece is built in over the bench next to the table, a conventional means of saving valuable floor space. Long rag runners stripe the floors of both houses, in typical Scandinavian style. Footed bread boards and other old implements in worn pine mix on the table, BELOW.

CHRISTMAS IN THE COUNTRY

Christmas is to winter what the Mid-summer holiday is to summer. All Scandinavia celebrates with great relish a festival of warmth and promise at the darkest moments of the year. The frosty white snow on high felt boots and wool caps, rosy cheeks, icy mustaches and beards, the blue light of early afternoon twilight and long indigo shadows on the ever-white ground, green-black spruces whose heavy boughs glow with little white lights—these are the signals of the season in the frozen north. Inside, firelight and candles twinkle everywhere to ward off the darkness and warm wintry homes and hearts.

Historically, Christmas was a time to make festive use of summer's bounty. Pre-served mushrooms, berries, cucumbers, and herring were fetched from the cellar, then soaked and dressed with sauces of soured and sweet cream or vinegar and spices. Hams, sausages, and meat loaves were prepared, using every part of a fresh-killed pig. And the house was filled with the smells of baking, as the big stone ovens turned out breads, cakes, cookies, and simple candies, such as preserved cranberries rolled in egg whites and powdered sugar.

The marvelous eighteenth-century home-stead of the Enbom family inspires them to re-create an old-fashioned Christmas in the Finnish countryside. Before the snow comes, the lingonberry and juniper branches must be picked and reindeer moss gathered to make decorations for indoors and out. A family ski outing into the forest just before the holiday will yield a tree that will be decked with apples, ginger, straw orna-ments, and other homemade objects. By the afternoon of Christmas Eve all is ready and the family will go to the churchyard to light candles in the snow at the graves of loved ones; this wonderful glowing vigil will be kept in wooded plots all over the country. A hot sauna is waiting at home, a 2,000-year-old Finnish ritual to make ready for celebra-tions, predating Christianity here by about 1,000 years. A hot *glögg* afterward is inter-rupted by a knock at the door: it is Father Christmas, who brings gifts in his burlap bag for everyone. The presents are opened and a many-course dinner is enjoyed by all.

In former times, Christmas was a twenty-day holiday and was danced away on the last night with more merrymaking and food. Now festivities have tapered down to a week: an eight-day family holiday is still a midwinter luxury all Scandinavians can af-ford. It is a time for feasting, greeting rela-tives, a sled ride to church, more eating, playing, and trying out new skates. Groaning boards of food are left out to greet hungry friends and family members who drop in. The celebrations end with a New Year's toast.

The restored farmhouse's entry is lit with candles in ice lanterns, in bowls of reindeer moss, and in small lamps forged of iron by Sten Enbom's father, LEFT *and* ABOVE. *A spruce with sparsely placed white lights glows at twilight's blue moment,* OPPOSITE.

Christmas is a festival of light, crafts, and treats. OPPOSITE: the children with Christmas Eve sparklers, handmade straw ornaments, a candle in a snowball lantern. LEFT: a hot waffle with cream and strawberry preserves, put up last summer, makes a delicious tree-trimming snack. ABOVE: fortunes are read in the poured lead that is melted in the fire on New Year's Eve.

PRECEDING PAGES: *coffee and baked goods fill a table in the farmhouse's "best room." A traditional straw goat peers at the table's goodies. Furnishings include a Finnish rococo corner cupboard and Queen Anne—type chairs.*

The tree, ABOVE LEFT, *is lit with real candles and decorated with homemade ornaments. Dinner, preceded by* glögg—*made of red wine laced with vodka and spiced with cloves, raisins, and almonds—is served in a log guesthouse,* ABOVE. *The panel hanging on the back wall is an old Danish tabletop. The meat table,* OPPOSITE, *is laid with cold salads and pork dishes garnished with prunes; turkey is a nontraditional addition.*

OVERLEAF: *a fruit-and-nut table stays set up in the dining room of the main house. Lots of candles light the place, including floating ones made in refrigerator egg trays. A collection of carved spinning-wheel distaffs, a traditional gift from a Finnish bridegroom to his fiancée, hang on the wall near a nineteenth-century painted corner cupboard.*

HOUSE OF MIRTH

The old stable with its faux fan windows, FAR LEFT, and a sundial, LEFT, on the grounds of the house. The home theatre, OPPOSITE, has the ring of summer make-believe. This set was painted by a Stockholm artist; two others were made by a member of the family.

OVERLEAF: sun streaming through an oak grove gives the manor a dappled appearance.

The magic of Lidingsberg is not only captured on the stage of her own vest-pocket theatre, but is felt everywhere on the premises of this landmark estate in Sweden. Built in three stages, starting in the late eighteenth century, the property seems caught in a trance. Yet it is still very much alive and shared by three generations of a family descended from the second owners. Dormant in the worst of winter, it comes to life seasonally—as it has since it was built—with the bustle of children on outings to the woods, of a couple of cousins cooking up good things in the kitchen, of the dog barking at guests who have come for dinner and a play.

The main house was bought as a summer home by a man from Stockholm, at a time when the island on which it stands was entirely wooded. Flanking freestanding wings were added in 1837, when the kitchen outbuilding was enveloped by a ballroom, study, and bedrooms, and in 1841, when another small cabin was enlarged by a new theatre. The consequent open-courtyard layout gives it the familiar appearance of many an ochre-painted Swedish country manor. The interiors reflect the periods of the various additions.

For parties, business associates and personal friends were brought over by boat from the city; plenty of extra bedrooms accommodated the guests. Musical evenings and plays provided stylish homegrown entertainment; all members of the family learned to perform. Today, the house holds joyful memories for those who can mark their lives in happy seasons spent there. Similar sentiments were expressed by an earlier family member who wrote of himself in third person when he recorded in a log book in 1871: "This year, 46 summers old. The other time doesn't count because summer at Lidingsberg has been his real life."

A corner of the south wing's ballroom with its set of Carl Johan (Swedish Empire) furniture and candelabra atop fluted columns, OPPOSITE and ABOVE. The simple wall-mounted table for serving contrasts with the grandeur of the setting. RIGHT: a writing table in a room in the same wing has a beautiful burl top and nineteenth-century mementoes.

The dining room furniture was painted white to lighten its look for summer use, in the fashion of the nineteenth century. A ship's painting on its stenciled walls, ABOVE, and period copper collection, LEFT. The decorative tile stove, FAR RIGHT, still heats the room on chilly days. A child's highchair, RIGHT, made in the early nineteenth century is from the province of Värmland.

CHAPTER TWO

BY THE WATER

As far back as Viking times, the waters of Scandinavia have served as avenues among northerly neighbors and to the world beyond. By the tenth century, the forbidding, pale-complected Norsemen of Norway, Sweden, and Denmark had sailed their stunning crafts to the British Isles, France, Germany, Spain, and as far as North Africa, Greece, and Persia. The North and Baltic sea trades would become important sources of livelihood for centuries, and rights to these waters were a much-disputed prize. Coastal life along the trade routes was blessed with rich seafood and commercial benefits, and was enhanced by knowledge from exotic civilizations.

In mainland areas, communication developed along watercourses as varied as the terrains of the different lands. The low-lying island kingdom of Denmark is surrounded by sea, save for the narrowest part of the peninsula that links her to the Continent. Her channels serve as the gateway to the Baltic and mark the invisible line between the salinity of the North Atlantic and the virtually sweet water of the Baltic. A ragged coast faces Norway toward the ocean and has afforded her long-lasting contact with the Anglo-Saxon world. Access to her lofty hinterlands was gained only by following the long fjords that reach from the sea into narrow valleys. Sweden's and Finland's shores are softened with an archipelago of thousands of islands whose make-up ranges from tough granite to meadows fit for grazing. And the lake country of Finland (and to a lesser extent that of Sweden), which was left in the wake of the Ice Age glaciers, provided an expansive network of watery highways for inland settlers. As if in pantheistic counterbalance to the rigors of life in such high latitudes, the warming waters of the Gulf Stream encircle the entire coast of Norway, keeping the sea open throughout the frozen winters and permitting farming even along the far-reaching fjords. Her neighbors also benefit from the drift of air heated over the warmer water, not a small factor in making life bearable in so northerly a clime. The frozen inland Baltic waters kept seaside Finland and Sweden cut off during the long winters until technology provided the know-how to build today's ice-breaking ships. On the other hand, frozen lakes and rivers there became solid surfaces across which villagers could easily sled or ski to destinations. Today, cars and skimobiles turn the several-meter-thick ice into convenient winter "roads."

Shanties, scattered homesteads, and towns grew up along shorelines, especially when fishing and transportation began to become important industries. Stockholm, for example, was founded by Baltic traders in the thirteenth century. The inlets of the sea lend a glittery, glamorous aspect to this island city and augment the quality of life in the "Venice of the north." Of much more humble nature

were the riverbank villages and scattered houses of the farmer-fishermen in the outlying regions of all five countries. Simple wood homes still face the water, a lasting testimony to the communication that it has offered in all weathers. Families in polar fishing villages, settlers who harvest nets full of seafood on coastal isles, and fruit growers who have staked out remote fjord valleys are all served by an elaborate network of steamers and mailboats now, too—reminders of the days when all outside news and transport reached Scandinavia's coasts in this form.

Founded by a Norwegian Viking, Ingolfur Arnarson, Iceland today is a nation whose economy depends on fishing. The everyday life of the island was lived very simply in isolated farmhouses or in small dwellings by the sea. The village of Heimey, on an island off the south coast, was visited by an itinerant Englishman in 1900 (it was later covered by ash in the volcanic eruption of 1969). His description of this fishing community probably remained accurate for decades thereafter: the shore was fronted by small wooden shanties where salted cod was stored at night; outdoor racks held strings of drying fish heads that clattered mysteriously in the wind. On posts hung oil lamps to guide fishermen who were out after dark—a rough but common undertaking in the winter months. Across a cobbled path stood the two-room huts of the fishermen's families, built low to the ground and made of piled turf and stones, or two-story cottages of wood and corrugated iron, most with sod roofs, too. Kitchen gardens, with patches of rhubarb, turnips, potatoes, and angelica added life and color. A simple, logical pattern organized the siting and construction of homes in such communities, granting villagers shared access to the sea and its resources. Their proximity to water dictated house proportions and building materials that would hold up in the fierce, changeable winds.

Even Denmark's more sheltered harbors taught the virtues of building low and close with sturdy, land-hugging materials like brick and timber, capped with the natural, bend-in-the-wind roofing of thatched sea grass. By the nineteenth century, successful Nordic merchants were seeking out seascapes for recreational living. Smart styles were interpreted in available materials, yet these descendants of fishermen followed native wisdom as to the shapes of structures and the sheltering advantages of natural harbors. Contemporary Scandinavians have since adapted such dwellings and still keep at least a rowboat, if not a sleeker sailing vessel, moored nearby for outings on light summer nights or for trips to a weekend house on a tiny offshore island. Even modern apartments seem to have inherited the seaman's penchant for creating shipshape interiors with careful wood fittings and clever storage solutions.

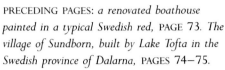

PRECEDING PAGES: *a renovated boathouse painted in a typical Swedish red,* PAGE 73. *The village of Sundborn, built by Lake Tofta in the Swedish province of Dalarna,* PAGES 74–75.

CLOCKWISE, FROM ABOVE: *a water lily in a rowboat on a lake in central Finland. A fisherman in the summery midnight sunset off the south coast of Norway. Bessastadir, the official home of the president of Iceland, shows the eighteenth-century architectural influence of the Danes who ruled the island then. The summer pavilion near a reflecting pool on the grounds of a manor house on the Danish island of Fyn. Flounder caught in local waters is smoked and sold by the fisherman's wife on Gullkrona, their island in the Finnish archipelago.*

A MARRIAGE OF TASTES

The island fortress of Vaxholmen was built by order of King Gustav Vasa of Sweden in 1548. A community to service it grew up on another small island a stone's throw away. Life in the village was not for the faint-hearted: as front-line defenders of the city of Stockholm, the inhabitants were required, until the twentieth century, to build their houses of wood and be prepared to tear them down in case of war. The picturesqueness of the place today—one of the closest to the mainland in the archipelago of islands that ripple out in concentric circles from the watery capital—owes its architectural continuity to the defensive building laws instituted by the monarch.

The home of John-Axel Johnson and Gladys Hultenby, like many in Scandinavia, comprises not one but a group of structures that step down a slope toward the Gulf of Bothnia. Ms. Hultenby, an interior architect, redesigned the main house along traditional lines on the site where a fisherman's cottage once stood. An old boathouse was renovated into a sauna; a log house at the top of the property has become a guesthouse; the old cold cellar carved into the hill near the kitchen door still serves its original purpose.

Their home is a marriage of different decorating tastes—his, romantic; hers, modern. Family antiques, nautical memorabilia, and twentieth-century classics strike an airy harmony. John-Axel, under Gladys's informed tutelage, has successfully resisted the collector's compulsion to fill the space with sentimental treasures. Instead, the house displays a warm yet spacious union of old and new. At its heart is an open kitchen with an inviting central hearth, of Gladys's design. In the old-world manner, it is used for both preparing food and heating and

offers the opportunity to cook over fragrant juniper or alder. There are curves and clean lines in every room, set off against masses of white, a typical Scandinavian device that prevents any sweetness from ever feeling syrupy. Here, whites look fresh in summer and dramatic against winter's pale landscape and dim light.

The house is sited at the very edge of the land, with Mr. Johnson's old wood skiff moored nearby, LEFT. *The courtyard created by the cluster of red cottages with crisp white trim has numerous small seating areas, as well as a sauna and garden.* OPPOSITE: *the gulf, seen past a model of Lord Nelson's ship,* Victory, *laps up to the living room, giving it the semblance of being at sea.*

OVERLEAF: *the stark simplicity of a long rag runner leading to an eighteenth-century Gustavian chair in the upstairs hall.* PAGE 81: *in both the kitchen,* ABOVE, *and living room,* BOTTOM LEFT, *there is a successful mix of pieces of good line from many periods. Above the cooking hearth hang drying bouquets of* éternelles *interspersed with duck decoys and copper pots. The sparsely furnished bedroom,* BOTTOM RIGHT, *seems to float on its own sea of tranquility. Its balcony opens onto a view of the islands that bob in the gulf.*

ON THE ROCKS

Rough lava stones are domesticated in the gabled end walls of Marbakki, LEFT and OPPOSITE. Their craggy texture sometimes calls for the contrasting delicacy of tubs of flowers placed nearby, and, at other turns, for an unusual collage of humble building materials and rock gardens blooming with a giant species of flower related to Queen Anne's lace.

Coastal property was always coveted in Iceland, for one of the gifts of the sea was the driftwood deposited on the shore. A treeless land dependent on natural handouts for building and fuel, Iceland looked to shipwrecks not only for precious wood but for other finery from the ships' cargoes. It was said long ago that some of the farmers who lived near the water prospered so from this bounty that they tied their horses with silk.

Marbakki is a house that looks out to sea from Álftanes, or Swan Peninsula, a bird-watcher's paradise only ten minutes from Reykjavik. Suburban houses here roost together on some of the land, and on another coastal stretch perches the official home of Iceland's president, a clean-lined white manor house built under Danish rule in the late eighteenth-century. Marbakki's gift from the sea is lava stone, which lay strewn about on the beach before a Norwegian soldier amassed it to build the gabled cottage and the turf-covered retaining wall that defends it from the tides. As the story goes, the Icelandic woman who owned the spit of land fell in love with the soldier during World War II. He made her a small home where they lived together, and he obtained wood from his native country to complete the interior.

Marín Magnusdóttir and Ólafur Schram bought the place in 1978 from an artist who had added a freestanding atelier a few yards from the cottage. They joined the structures by means of a wide passage-cum-kitchen/dining room that made the two buildings into an L-shaped home. Plentiful use of tongue-and-groove paneling unites the artist's all-wood former studio (now children's rooms and den) with the pitched-ceiling cottage (the master bedroom and living room). Varied paint and stain treatments keep the new sections from saunalike woodiness. Walls of windows bring an expanse of lawn and endless sea into sight.

An ex post facto decorating scheme took its cue from the artist's whitewash-and-bottle-green scheme and diluted its high contrast with stripped pine cupboards and recycled wood fittings from local shops and a pub. Relaxed rooms—which either sleep two cozily or easily seat the family of five, two golden retrievers, and then some—are the comfortable result. The large kitchen/dining space attests to Marín's culinary expertise—based, like her decorating skill, on personal versions of local specialties—and to the natural gravitation of family and friends to the core of the house.

OVERLEAF: *the house's entry hall,* PAGE 84, *introduces the mix of woods that dominates its interior.* PAGE 85: *the ceiling of the dining room addition follows a slope that ties it to the lines of the original cottage. Thin pancakes are the hallmark of a good Icelandic cook; they are rolled in sugar or filled with homemade jam and whipped cream. The master bedroom is a Mondrian-like composition of planes of color.*

The Craft of Living

The simple, mortar-washed brick façade, FAR LEFT, *conceals the open interior space with its spectacular sea vista. Windows are pierced in the deep walls to control the view, not splash it all around.* OPPOSITE: *model ships, telescopes, and old spoke-back chairs are integrated into the modern mix,* TOP. *The patina of family use enriches a classic dining table and chairs by Danish architect Finn Juhl,* BOTTOM RIGHT.

Through the Øresund Strait, the narrows between North Zealand in Denmark and the Skåne peninsula of Sweden, passes all the sea traffic bound for the Baltic. On a clear day Sweden is easily visible from the Danish shore, and at night the lights along the flat coast there shine like a string of diamonds. A house cantilevered on the hill follows the coast on the Danish side, offering a splendid view of commercial and pleasure boats and affording a kind of privacy to its owners that comes from being a notch or two above most of your neighbors. A deck that runs the full length of the rectangular house on the downhill side and wraps around the kitchen provides several quiet seating and dining areas; screens and plantings shelter it from sea winds. On the uphill side, two bamboo and gravel gardens offer more protected spaces to take a meal or nap in a hammock.

Privacy is only one of the issues to which architect Jørgen Møller was sensitive in designing this home for Torben and Kirstin Ørskov in 1979. Entertaining plays a role in the Ørskovs' professional and private lives; in their thirty years of design consultation, manufacturing, and wholesaling, their home has frequently served as a showcase for their trades. Many of the items that furnish the rooms are objects that Torben commissioned from designers and architects who became friends. One of these is Møller, whose watches and thermometer for Royal Copenhagen now figure in museum design collections. He gave the Ørskovs a home—adapted from the sure proportions of a Danish farmhouse and made of the same modest materials—that is open for guests but whose warm, natural substance promotes feelings of closeness for just one or two. The house's lower floor, designed with then-teenaged children in mind, functions as a separate apartment—a space that honored the adolescents' privacy and now respects that of overnight guests. Thoughtful detailing on slatted ceilings, windows, stone floors, and cabinetry confirm the craftsmanlike quality of Møller's work.

The understated quality of the kitchen's design reinforces this room's continuity with the living/dining space. Here, clever detailing makes furniture-finish counters of bowling-alley flooring; childproof burners of cooking elements, set back from the edge of the work surface; useful deep niches for refrigerator/freezer, glassware, and so on, OPPOSITE and ABOVE. Shrimp with dill cooking for lunch, RIGHT.

IN CHEKHOVIAN SPLENDOR

A romantic retreat by the water's edge has been a summer home to four generations of a Finnish family brought up near the coast. In the late nineteenth century, when the nearest town, Pori, was the largest export harbor in the country, three shipping families from there bought neighboring properties to provide their children with the seasonal pleasure of a fresh-air lifestyle. Honkala, a yellow wood house with white trim, still stands in Chekhovian splendor in a grove of birches. This dacha style keeps aesthetically alive the nineteenth-century, when Finland was an autonomous grand duchy of tsarist Russia.

Now, for not quite half the year, Maire Gullichsen lives at Honkala and transports herself to an era reminiscent of her childhood and that of her mother and her children. Such continuity is as much a source of delight as the idle hours and light nights passed at this lovely estate. "Everything that's a part of life has happened in this house," she muses. "Marriages, the christening of children . . . I was even born here." (The family was having dinner when the midwife opened the double doors of an adjoining room to announce the birth.)

The creamery colors of the house's exterior are echoed in the pale interior rooms, made even paler with lots of white. Dark wood furniture was painted over and wall-coverings were chosen with long, radiant summer days in mind. Textiles came from the Home Craft Shop—one of those started in parts of Scandinavia, about the time the house was built, as a way to preserve traditional farm skills. Two bedrooms, a sleeping/sitting room, and a sun porch that spans the back of the house radiate off the large, light-filled living/dining room. Upstairs, more bedrooms fan off a central hall in a similar plan. Mrs. Gullichsen fondly remembers the evenings of her name day, when she would throw yellow roses down to serenading callers—and the summer nights when she escaped down a rope ladder (required by law in upper rooms in case of fire) "without Father knowing."

Life in earlier times revolved around summer theatre—members of the family acted in the nearby company—crayfish parties, evening readings, and the like. Play-houses with Lilliputian porches, gardens, yards, and several rooms, were built for the children. The sauna and smokehouse still sit by the sea near a triangular dock that floats like the water lilies in the sheltered cove. Fern-lined paths continue over white bridges, leading to a cherry tree or a patch of strawberries and milky flowers beyond a milky gate. Swings on the grounds still provide places to steal away with a good book, and groupings of tables and chairs furnish several spots for outdoor socializing. A small, rose-covered garden pavilion is an appealing place to take tea on cool nights or lazy afternoons.

Honkala's gardens, LEFT, include a delightful pavilion, OPPOSITE, referred to as the Goethe House because of the walls, which Finnish artist Tove Jansson painted with stories from Goethe as a gift for Maire Gullichsen's fortieth birthday.

OVERLEAF: the living room's pale yellows are a foil for a romantic scarlet pouf that was made from old sugar crates. The children have always played hide-and-seek underneath this piece of furniture, which can be pulled apart like plump pie slices and moved into the four corners of the room for dances.

PRECEDING PAGES: *blues and whites complement creamery yellows elsewhere—the wainscoted front hall* (PAGE 94) *and wash-corner of a bedroom* (PAGE 95).

A romantic portrait of Mrs. Gullichsen's mother, pregnant with her first child, hangs over an overstuffed sofa on the sun porch, RIGHT. Woven blue linen runners add depth to the corner bedroom where the current owner was born, ABOVE.

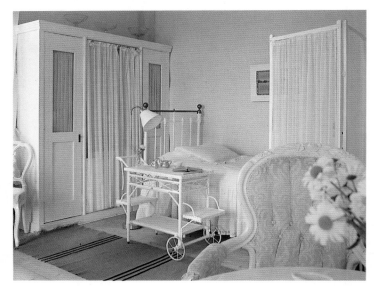

OPPOSITE, CLOCKWISE FROM TOP LEFT: *a samovar presides on a dining-area console; one of Mrs. Gullichsen's romantic garden bouquets; the strict lines of the dining room's Gustavian table and chairs are made fanciful by a white organdy lampshade and curtains; a spacious bedroom/sitting room; peering into a bedroom past the dining corner's painted clock and highchair; the view from a window is colored by vivid begonias and lush greens.*
ABOVE: *Honkala is shielded from the sea by a stand of tall birches. The flying of the flag signifies that the family is at home. A sauna cabin by the water enables heating sessions followed by refreshing dips; nearby benches are for taking the air afterward.*

Outdoor Orientation

Native and planted greens embellish the Nurmesniemi house outdoors and in. OPPOSITE: *Antti's wire benches and Vuokko's softly weathered cottons catch the light on the seaside deck,* TOP. *Two table set-ups are topped with the strong prints for which Vuokko is known: one in the dining room is surrounded by Antti's leather and chrome chairs; another is outdoors, beside a copper beech tree and garden path.*

Entertaining is a great part of Antti and Vuokko Nurmesniemi's personal and professional lives. The couple—he an architect/industrial designer, she a textile artist/fashion designer—share very full work-related lives. They often collaborate with others in home studios, show their new lines in the open interior spaces, planned with this use in mind, and frequently invite colleagues for cocktails or dinner to compare notes. Moreover, they are often called on to open their home to foreign dignitaries, as a model of the architecture and design acumen that has earned Finland its high reputation in international circles. Both Antti and Vuokko are gold-medal winners at Milan Triannales, the world's fairs of design, and recipients of the Lunning Prize, conferred by the founder of Georg Jensen on noted Scandinavian designers.

The Nurmesniemis' home by the Gulf of Finland is within eight minutes of Helsinki's neoclassical-style city hall. Antti has sited the clean wood-and-glass structure as low as possible so that its lines don't impose on the natural horizon. Native pines, sea grasses and wildflowers are supplemented by plantings of blackberry bushes, leafy ground cover, and stalky English flowers. A rear wood deck takes advantage of the sea's proximity.

A chalky-clean interior changes hue with chameleonlike flexibility as the sun wraps around the house's window walls at different times of the day. In summer, intense greens tint the white strutwork-supported ceilings, while the reflected gleam of sunlight on the sea sometimes sets the walls shimmering. Winter's icy cloak bleaches out the whites, vividly outlining Vuokko's textiles against Antti's furniture designs. An elegant simplicity, akin to that of the Japanese, characterizes the interiors and the arrangements of fresh leaves, set against natural wood or white surfaces.

PAINTER'S PLEASURE

Hans Dahl was one of a handful of artists who came to make their homes in the late nineteenth century in Balestrand, a village on Norway's longest fjord. He was seduced by the valley of clear light and the receding planes of mountains that rise from the water ever more abruptly as the fjord extends inland some 110 miles from the Norwegian Sea. His timber villa, like several others in the town, was clad in wood paneling ornamented with motifs reinterpreted from Norway's remarkable carved-Viking-ship and stave-church tradition. This hybrid look was dubbed "dragon style" for the mythological animal heads—ancient symbols used to ward off evil spirits—applied to roof peaks and cupula corners. The romantic revival style, found on turn-of-the-century houses, hotels, and some churches, represented a celebration of cultural roots by a people eager to gain national independence from the then-ruling Swedes.

Artist Dahl took the look a few playful steps further. Beyond the brackets, balustraded balconies, and jigsaw trim, he carved a covey of coy faces into the window frames and porch posts, animating the colorful façade and relieving the fierceness of the dragon motifs.

Dahl brought color of a different kind to the village when Kaiser Wilhelm II of Germany, whom he had met while studying abroad, paid him a visit in the summer of 1914. Kaiser Wilhelm arrived on a three-stack steamer accompanied by a flotilla of twenty-four warships, all of which laid anchor in the fjord just off the house's dock. Afternoon waltzes were held in the garden—the entourage traveled with its own musicians—and a bevy of Bergen beauties was imported by boat for the not inconsequential numbers of handsome young officers that made the journey. The kaiser took to walking his six dogs with bells on in the village each day. And when a local home caught fire he mustered his ships' hoses to help battle the blaze. In a final gesture of good will he had erected on a promontory across the fjord a 42-meter statue of Fridtjov, the saga personnage whose love for a local maiden was legendary.

Representational and geometric carvings adorn the façade on windows, doors, balconies, roof peaks. Overhanging structure, and the use of many verandas and projections gives houses of the period an alpine appearance, sometimes referred to as the Swiss style, OPPOSITE.

CLASSIC HARMONY WITH NATURE

I have been called a neorationalist, a post-modernist," says Danish architect Claus Bonderup. But he resists such tags or any others that imply he is one of those who claim to have left modernism behind. "Modernists took our architectural history away. Now some of us are trying to put it back. I don't think we abandoned modern. I think we are making it richer."

Bonderup's way of interpreting his heritage is to open himself to the currents of architecture, as Danes always have, refining and adapting to make forms suitable to his native land. His projects in Egypt, Australia, Brazil, the United States, and Scandinavia, expose him to ideas from around the globe. A kinship with Scandinavian sensibilities grounds him in practices that work at home.

The calm proportions and cool balance of the house Bonderup designed for himself ten years ago on Denmark's west coast reflect his admiration for Nordic classicism, itself an aesthetic acquisition from southern Europe in the early nineteenth century. Digging into the dunes, he fashioned a half-underground house whose ordered plan is as vital to the environment through its discretion as the surroundings are in giving life to its interior. The three-part, poured-concrete construction is insulated by the dunes. Partial domes, like large, unblinking eyes, open it up toward the sea and focus on an uninterrupted view of the coast while drawing in the clear northwestern light. A square module articulates each of the three sections—a clean reduction of the house's geometry to simplest forms. As in some of the best Scandinavian architecture, therein lies its structural strength and its power to please.

An interior of white-painted concrete floors, walls, and ceilings acts as a mass to store the afternoon sun's heat and also as a canvas for reflected sunsets. Many of Bonderup's own furniture and lighting designs are set around the 120-square-meter space. His precise arrangements, even for amusing tablescapes, prove he is a builder by nature and a classicist at heart.

Looking from the kitchen toward the dining dome, ABOVE LEFT, *exposed ductwork and Bonderup's free-form screen design make a minimal statement all in white. The kitchen's vaulted ceiling,* ABOVE, *follows the lines of the glasswork it faces. Domed projections create dune-rooms,* OPPOSITE.

OVERLEAF: *the neatly camouflaged house takes in a Jutland sunset.*

Reflected light plays on the surface of the glass and interior, ABOVE and
LEFT. OPPOSITE: *The architect's projects, past and future, line up along a
wall that runs from the slatted flooring of the open garage to a study,* TOP;
*they include an arctic-night rendering of a library that won a competition
in northern Finland, skis, chair, and lamps. Bonderup's tablescapes are
compositions of working models, renderings, and things at hand:* RIGHT, *the
study table and a terrace, seen through glass doors;* FAR RIGHT, *a kitchen-
counter still life.*

FRESHWATER FEAST

Crayfish are arranged in a spiral on a platter and topped with a crown of dill flowers. A schnapps bottle, served in a block of ice, keeps its cool for first-course toasts; currant leaves freshen the water in a fingerbowl. OPPOSITE: a cloth of sea blues by Finlayson covers the built-in table. A garden and wildflower bouquet makes a natural centerpiece.

Crayfish parties pleasurably extend a short summer. The freshwater crustaceans are fished from lakes and rivers in Norway, Sweden, and Finland starting in late July. They find their way to tabletops in restaurants and homes and are especially delectable outdoors during the long, light nights. Romantic wooden gazebos with carpenter cutouts from the end of the nineteenth century are put to use for leisurely dinners that start with crayfish prepared in a bath of water, dill, and spices and served cold. The custom is one schnapps—icy vodka or akvavit—for each shellfish, so guests are likewise well watered as the ritual continues. Morsels topped with sprigs of dill and chased with toasts lead to more and more crayfish until the platter is bare. Beer accompanies the feast. A breeze wafts the scent of pine and wildflowers toward diners in this setting on Finland's south coast.

By Hand

Built on a bay as a bath house by British troops stationed in Iceland during World War II, this small structure found use as a stable at the war's end. When the Ragnarssons, who now live here, took it over in 1952, their own displacement by the war may have made them look kindly on the humble concrete-block building. A from-the-ground-up renovation that took more than five years saw them living in the kitchen, the first room to be completed, for a full twelve months. They fashioned rooms out of the open stable space, and stuccoed and painted outer walls. A corrugated iron roof was added, and a front porch was attached with exposed timber posts. Later, trees and flower beds were planted to make a proper yard, and a field of wildflowers was sown beyond the wooden fence.

The scale of the cottage, its pink-washed walls with deep-green roof, and the attention given its small garden are clues to the Danish upbringing of Mrs. Ragnarsson. Paul Ragnarsson's life at sea, as a commercial sailor and later as a chartmaker, shows in his know-how for building in close quarters with available supplies. Two bedrooms and a bath on the second floor make optimal use of the space under the eaves with low built-in furniture. Downstairs, the compact kitchen can seat six for dining and, in the open living room, groupings of furniture and artwork visually divide the space. Throughout the house, his ship's art, her flowers, his workmanship, her orderly arrangement of Danish and Swedish furniture, interspersed with a few Icelandic pieces, makes for a his-and-hers effort as disarming and genuine as the house's origins.

The cottage is seen across wildflower meadows, a pastoral surprise in volcanic Iceland, TOP. *An inner yard,* ABOVE, *is planted with flower beds and deciduous trees that give it a sense of privacy in the wide-open terrain.* OPPOSITE: *an Icelandic dragon-style chair in a corner of the living room alludes to the Viking origins of the island,* TOP. *The desk is Danish; the miniature copper kettles, Swedish. The kitchen,* RIGHT; *a bedroom corner,* FAR RIGHT.

OVERLEAF: *the stairs were built and railings carved by the owner. The stove that heats the house is decoratively integrated with collected objects.*

C H A P T E R   T H R E E

OVER THE MEADOWS

Rolling wintry-white pastures and sunny summer meadows offer a cultivated contrast to the more rugged wilderness regions of Scandinavia. Only the rich soils of Denmark and southern Sweden took readily to tilling. The beguiling gentle landscapes of these areas, still largely agricultural, belie the difficulty with which land was readied for farming on poorer ground farther north. Clearing timber and draining bogs or soil saturated annually in the thaw of melting snows comprised the primary tasks in much of central Sweden and Finland. Norway's farmers eked out a living in the narrow river valleys that run like great long fingers to the sea and served as the major routes of travel through the mountainous countryside. And large tracts in Iceland, blessed by plains of wild grasses, though not much else, were turned into grazing land for horses and sheep. Here, too, farms sprang up along fertile river valleys or on land spared the pitting and pummeling of volcanic eruption. Everywhere, workable land was held precious and was passed along from father to son.

Although the degree of comfort on a particular farm varied considerably with its size and output, farm life in all the Scandinavian countries bred a kind of craftsmanship and a sense of community different from those in the wilder regions. Good fellowship among freeholding farmers—and systems for collecting grain to distribute to needy families during difficult years and for pooling dairy products for processing—planted the seeds of the social consciousness that was to affect the area's political life in later years. Sprawling homesteads, consisting of many freestanding or interconnected buildings, sheltered not only the farm owner and his family, but also laborers and their wives and children. In outlying provinces, people even slept together in large dormitory-style rooms, with curtained bed-closets built for only the master and mistress of the house. In Iceland, for instance, a dark winter's afternoon on an isolated farm would find all members of the extended farm "family" burrowed underground, congregated in one of the warren of rooms in the turf house, listening to lessons by lamplight, with whittling or textile work in their laps. A long tradition of oral recitation in that country accounts not only for the preservation of the great sagas—more than just good stories, they give a literal history of the country in the first few centuries after its settlement—but also for the education of the peasant classes in places where schools were nonexistent. In Norway, Sweden, and Finland storytelling was also a popular evening pastime that accompanied handwork and contributed to the great bodies of mythology from those places.

A well-to-do landowner in Sweden might have his own sawmill, a flour mill, a dairy, a small iron mine, and a workroom with looms where the tenant farmers' and laborers' wives each took shifts at weaving during the day. From his timber the structures and furniture for all the farm buildings were made. An itinerant carpenter or skilled villager might craft the nicest pieces for the main house, copying from traditional patterns or fine models brought back from travels to the capital. From the owner's fields came the flax and hemp that were spun and woven into textiles for practical use and decoration. The iron mine furnished the metal to make all-important knives and tools. (The color of the wooden farm buildings was a by-product of the local copper mines. The mines in central Sweden are said to belong to some of the oldest mining companies in the world, founded in the twelfth century. Near one mine in the province of Dalarna, a goat that had turned up half dyed red was discovered to have rubbed up against rocks containing copper that had been oxidized by the air and a forest fire. The pigment was found to be an excellent wood preservative and outlasted paint when applied to buildings.)

Self-sufficiency characterized life on every farm, grand or poor, and taught Nordics the skills and love of home that led to their proficiency in the domestic arts when industrialization came. Today's high-quality cotton textiles, rag rugs, light wood furniture in both neoclassical and provincial styles, wooden field-lunch implements, cutlery, wood-stave baskets, and so on, are legacies of the old agricultural lifestyle.

In Finland, Sweden, and Norway, the manor houses of the first landed gentry were simply log constructions made along conventional lines and then prettied up with board-and-batten exteriors as sawn boards became available. The great homes of Denmark, however, were fashioned to suit more baronial tastes, reflecting the influence of the nearby Continent. The more modest and typical Danish farmhouse style developed to suit the materials at hand and had a much greater impact on how people came to live, even when construction methods grew more sophisticated. This island realm with limited land at its disposal made its forests go farther by using the half-timbering technique to build farm homes. A wooden framework created a system of square modules that were filled in with mud and sticks; the deep-stained timbers were left exposed, while the filler spaces were whitewashed. Simple daub-and-wattle filling eventually gave way to bricks when that material became widely available and desirable for its resistance to fire. The skeletal half-timber structure set up a network of bays where windows and doors could be positioned and dictated the proportion of all buildings built in this way, from homes to barns. The technique was adaptable to structures of all sizes; more modules were simply added to suit the need. The clean, closed volumes, with their predictable rhythm of bays, trained the Danes' eyes to the harmonious proportions that have been applied to more recent architecture and that today give an admired consistency to the residential and public buildings of different periods there. The court- and terrace-style houses perfected by internationally recognized Danish architects such as Arne Jacobsen and Jørn Utzøn in the post–World War II years owe a debt to the balance and regularity of the agrarian style of centuries before.

PRECEDING PAGES: *the interior of a barn at Grythyttan, in the Swedish province of Varmland,* PAGE 117; *grasses and flowers have been left to dry after the Midsummer festivities. Later, they will serve as indoor winter decorations. Icelandic Toelt horses follow the lead horse across a plain,* PAGES 118—119. *The breed has remained pure since it was introduced from Norway in the tenth century.*

CLOCKWISE, FROM ABOVE: *the popularity of all-natural modern textiles grew out of the Scandinavian farm weaving heritage; here, a cotton print by Fujiwo Ishimoto for Marimekko. A seventeenth-century painted armoire and eighteenth-century Gustavian chairs from a farm manor in central Sweden. A half-timber Danish barn with thatched roof; modules established by the framing method give balance to the proportions of buildings constructed in this way, and to those derived from agrarian models in later years. Haystacks in interior Finland. A built-in Swedish bed closet with farm weavings and painted clock.*

ALL THAT MEETS THE EYE, AND MORE

In the fertile valleys of Skåne lie some of the most alluring picture-book farms of Scandinavia. Part of Denmark until the mid-seventeenth century, Sweden's southernmost province was a lovely and agriculturally productive trophy won by the more northerly nation in a battle that took the Danes by surprise. King Charles X of Sweden capitalized on an extremely cold winter and marched his 7,000 mounted troops over the ice covering the narrow straits that link the islands of Denmark with each other and nearby Skåne.

The cobbled-courtyard form of the provincial farms of Skåne stem from their former allegiance to Denmark, as well as climatic conditions more akin to those of nearby Zealand than those of northern Sweden. Here, farms were built to withstand the wind that whines from the west through

Denmark and across the tip of the Swedish peninsula. Thatched straw was found to resist its force better than tile or slate, both of which were later adopted for city structures. Positioning a house on an east-west axis lessened the blustery impact, and turning all the buildings in on themselves created a protected enclosure.

The oldest part of the typical half-timber farm shown here was constructed not long after the Swedish conquest. Additions were made over the next two centuries, brick and wood clapboard updating the accustomed materials for barn and outbuildings. Sixteen years ago, when Ingemar Tunander and his wife purchased the place, they patched the main building's deteriorating walls and replaced the roof with fresh thatch, which now will last for twenty-four more seasons.

The tidy appearance of the working farm belies the urbanity of its interior. The Tunanders have secured for themselves an inner domain in which collected furnishings from all periods have been arranged with a careful hand and a knowing eye. Both art historians by training, the ex-curator and writer have succeeded in making spatial sense of the long, tricky, box of a house. Key to their success are the items, whether provincial or fine, of infallible line and interesting finish, set about with more dash than usual antique assemblages admit. Precious stone pieces are placed side by side with trompe-l'oeil updates. Collector's-item wallcoverings give character to secondary spaces. Perhaps most important is the everyday use to which these possessions are put, no matter what the vintage, in a manner that makes for an inviting home without overly inflating the value of its one-of-a-kind contents.

Traditional half-timber construction sets up a rhythm of bays that dictates the pleasing proportions of all such buildings, LEFT. OPPOSITE: *the farm nestles in a bend of a dirt road that gives access only to its fields and a neighbor,* TOP. *Light falls through the courtyard onto the front hall floor, made of stones that were found in the garden and are thought to be originally from a local church,* BOTTOM. *Chest and clock from the central Swedish province of Dalarna team up with an eighteenth-century chair and paintings and nineteenth-century wallcoverings.*

The narrow dining room is fitted with a stunning, late-seventeenth-century, leather-topped table, painted Baroque chairs, and a glass lamp designed in the 1920s by Swedish architect Gunnar Asplund, OPPOSITE. The leather cover is treated with wax, like a saddle; dining spills add to its mottled appeal. In a kitchen corner, ABOVE, a farmer's footstool-chair sidles up to a 300-year-old table and painted pieces of various vintages. Decanters of white and homemade elder wines, RIGHT, are placed near a Ming bowl on an eighteenth-century limestone table, whose patina is maintained with a paste of butter and red wine.

At one end of the living room a faux tile stove has been painted by Mr. Tunander to match the real one that faces it at the room's other end, ABOVE. Comfortably worn linen and pale leather cover eighteenth-century chairs. In a niche created by built-in bookcases, LEFT, a Swedish Empire (Carl Johan style) table with its griffen motif has a faux marble base and real porphyry top. OPPOSITE: more of the couple's collection of porphyry, a hard Egyptian stone containing feldspar crystals. Here, it is filled with faux wood fruit; the console table was hand-painted by the owner in eight blues and greens on an umber ground.

OVERLEAF: classical furnishings in porphyry, metal, and wood reiterate motifs in the unusual scenic nineteenth-century Swedish wallpaper of a romantic bath and dressing room.

LIVING IN THE PAST

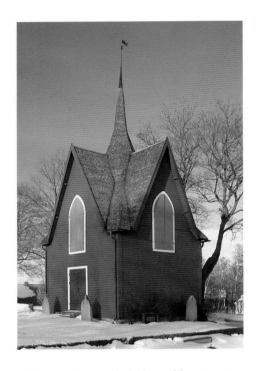

Entering Olivehult is like stepping back into a time when gentlemen and ladies at a summer party promenaded through a park of pines or rowed to the small island in the lake, when timber and grain were harvested on the 25,000-hectare farm, when home-woven linens were washed and cold-pressed through a mangle with stone-weighted wood rollers—because life is still lived in this way to a certain extent at this seventeenth-century Swedish estate. Built in 1640 as a log manor, the structure was given a second floor and its distinctive mansard roof a hundred years later by a man from whom the present owners are descended. Mr. Linnerhjelm became celebrated as Sweden's first map maker. The manor house bears his coat of arms over the door, his Rousseauesque vi-sion of surrounding park and gardens, and the splendid style of his furnishings inside.

The interior is an ode to Scandinavian interpretations of Continental motifs, characteristic of the grandest look of the day. But its special charm derives from an imaginative color sense and the knowing play of the ornamental against the plain. Dominant deep ochres, greens, and browns are offset by bleached pine floors or groupings of pale furniture, casting many of the rooms in a rich mix of shadow and light. Embossed-leather and painted-linen wallcoverings are thought to have been sent for from Holland; furniture was brought from Stockholm, where King Gustaf III set the style after the late eighteenth-century French and English lines he so admired. Even in the most formal rooms, provincial Swedish touches, like the flashed-tile stoves and unadorned linen curtains, counter the potential heaviness of the courtly pieces.

The kitchen was moved inside the main house in the nineteenth century; it had previously been housed in an outbuilding in the back. The original pantry, still intact, hints at the elegance of the country evenings at the manor. Hunting parties were often organized in autumn, and the finest warm-weather soirees are said to have been given at the turn of the century by the nieces of the last Linnerhjelm.

The manor house's board-and-batten exterior, OPPOSITE, *covers walls built of logs. It is built in the Carolinean style, named for Charles XII, Sweden's heroic warrior-king.* ABOVE LEFT: *the wooden country church serves a neighborhood parish. Outbuildings—like this monumental hay barn—and animals enrich the atmosphere of the farm property,* ABOVE.

OVERLEAF: *original eighteenth-century leather wallcoverings, embroidered linens, and gilded Rococo furniture add grandeur to the master bedroom,* PAGE 132, TOP AND BOTTOM LEFT. *The Scandinavian tradition for simplicity takes a classical stance in an extra bedroom with its built-in* cabinet de toilette, BOTTOM RIGHT, *and fuses utility with beauty in the manor's entry hall,* PAGE 133.

PRECEDING PAGES: *the icy elegance of this print room is warmed with touches of brass, gilt frames, and carvings on the furniture,* PAGES 134–135. *Copper engravings of the Swedish countryside are by an early nineteenth-century artist called Martin. The living room's remarkable oil paintings of Biblical scenes are thought to have been moved upstairs during the eighteenth-century remodeling of the house because the tales are not hung in order,* PAGES 136–137. *Here, the Old Testament story of Esther is portrayed near a Swedish piano with candlestand from about 1800.*

Daytime winter candlelight illumines the print room's cool, classic fittings, ABOVE LEFT. *The rich blue tiled stove contrasts unusually with the browns, greens, and golds of the master bedroom,* ABOVE. OPPOSITE: *the living room's dark painted walls are set off by pale Gustavian furnishings,* TOP. *The center table is a nineteenth-century addition. Pattern on pattern is a decorative surprise in some of the print room's furnishings; the photo albums date from the nineteenth century. Eighteenth-century fittings still line the walls of the pantry; here, Swedish pewter and English-inspired pottery tureens.*

Handsome painted-linen walls give a sophisticated air to the fresh white-and-wood dining room, ABOVE AND OPPOSITE. The furniture is Gustavian. Moss between sets of windows is the traditional method for blocking drafts and absorbing humidity, BELOW.

Buried Treasures

Iceland's picturesque turf architecture puts us as close as we can come to imagining the earliest dwellings in the northern lands; besides the Icelanders, only the semi-nomadic Lapps, who live in a boundaryless territory across the top of Norway, Sweden, and Finland, still put sod structures to limited use. Grassy knolls on the horizon are easily taken as yet another unexplained natural outcropping on the often-surrealistic Icelandic terrain. But up close, one reads regular spaces within the mounds and perceives the logic that connected the underground rooms and secured them against the gales that sweep over the country, indiscriminate in the beating they inflict on every upright surface on the treeless island.

Thanks to the preservative properties of volcanic ash, which blanketed some farms during an eruption in about 1100, ruins have been excavated that validate theories of how the sod buildings evolved to the shapes they acquired by the early twentieth century, when many were still in use. Inside the thick earth walls, wooden-stave construction made surprisingly roomy living places of some of the farmsteads. What started out as a large single-room hall, where fires burned in the middle of the floor, gradually gave way to a group of rooms with separate functions. In time, a plan evolved in which a row of front rooms was turned end-out, creating a distinctive zigzag of gables. At the better farms, the gabled ends were dressed with painted board and batten. An equation could be made between the prosperity of the property and the number of painted peaks that fronted its earthy forms. The examples here, although not lived in today, are seasonally open to visitors, and many are furnished as they were when they housed the last of their owners.

The chief building materials were turf, stone, and wood, which drifted ashore or was imported. Readily available and easily portable, turf was either stacked in strips or laid in a tight-fitting herringbone pattern. ABOVE: *a gabled end of the vicarage at Laufás, renovated several times since it was first built in the sixteenth century. A re-creation of the medieval farm at Stöng,* OPPOSITE TOP. *One of the best of its day, it was covered with ash in the eruption of Mount Hekla in 1104.*

OPPOSITE AND OVERLEAF: *the farm at Glaumbaer, whose oldest portions date to the eighteenth century, with its row of gabled front rooms and back-hall peak topped with carved, crossed Viking horns.*

IN PRAISE OF HOME

Were he alive today, Carl Larsson would have reason to be a contented man. For he realized his intention—to make a model of happy home life—at Little Hyttnäs, the extraordinary cottage he and his wife, Karin, fashioned for themselves in the Swedish province of Dalarna. More celebrated outside Sweden for the artistry of his house and the delightful watercolors he made there of his wife and seven children than he is for his murals and oils, Carl Larsson lived a life that symbolized, at least in its depiction, the ideals of the Arts and Crafts movement, of which he was a disciple. If he was guilty of painting too rosy a picture of his domestic-artistic bliss, it is because he found in this lifestyle both the fulfillment of a "progressive" philosophy that venerated old-fashioned ideals and a compensation for his own terribly unhappy childhood.

The combined vision and skills of Carl and Karin Larsson turned a log cabin inherited in 1889 into an agreeably rambling studio/house where the large family learned the pleasures and practice of good cooking, sewing, weaving, gardening, sketching, and home decorating. Influenced by the illustrative wall paintings of local eighteenth-century farmhouses, several years spent together at an artists' colony in France, and the growing popular rejection of the bourgeois style of the new industrialists, the two personalized nearly every surface of every room of their home.

In 1899, Larsson published a book of twenty-four watercolors of the place, annotated with bits of folkloric self-wisdom. It met with almost immediate success, for not only did it justify the belief that a lovely home and family were the routes to the good life, but it showed how to achieve happiness with country-carpenter furniture, a paintbrush and clear color, unmatched family hand-me-downs, and a patchwork approach to architecture that glorified small, cozy rooms. It became, in the words of writer Ulf Hård af Segerstad, "the national home" of Sweden. If Larsson never achieved the far-reaching prominence as a fine artist that he desired, he did become a laureate of the art of living.

Carl and Karin Larsson's house, in an idyllic lakeside setting surrounded by farmland, shows the artist's idiosyncratic use of color and texture under the influence of the English Arts and Crafts style. A well is decoratively enclosed; the swag motif is also found in interior painting. In the dining room, OPPOSITE, are Karin's modernistic tapestry work—a testimony to World War I—on the high-back bench, Carl's paper-cutout lamp, and boldly painted reproduction Gustavian chairs made by a local carpenter. One of many portraits of their children is painted on the door.

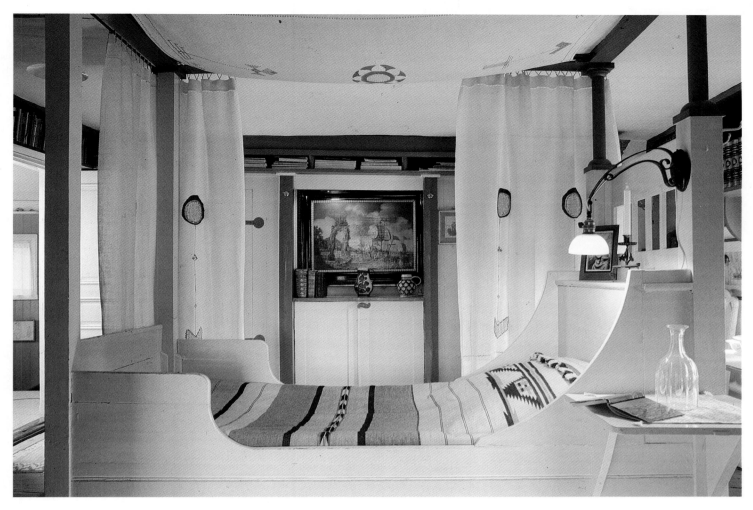

OPPOSITE: *fine oak paneling from the seventeenth century was recycled in the "Old Room," a guest bedroom named for its marvelous mélange of antiques that includes Flemish paintings and an eighteenth-century Swedish ceiling lantern—all of which were put to practical use. The bed closet was cleverly made in the Larssons' own version of the traditional country treatment.* ABOVE: *Carl's bedroom with its unconventional floating bed and handsomely spare woven textiles by Karin. Repainted spice cabinet from the "Old Room,"* RIGHT.

Most recognizably Swedish is the light-filled living room, with its fresh blue-and-white cottons, inherited Gustavian chairs softened with plaid petticoatlike covers, and ivies trained to frame the windows, LEFT. It was constantly used by the family for doing lessons, chatting over coffee, or sitting in the sunlight in cold weather. ABOVE: a corner of the nursery end of Karin's bedroom, with its high ceilings, swag-and-bow border, and one child's bed, "ingeniously made of pine chip [a roofing material], according to my wife's foolish suggestion," noted Carl.

At the other end of Karin's sleeping room, a decorative tile stove, and the room's painted dedication on her name day, when the decorating was complete, RIGHT. One of her hangings draws across the door to her husband's room. Her weaving and sewing corner, ABOVE. When Carl's painting demanded more space and quiet, and a larger studio was built, this original studio became a crafts room for the whole family.

PRE-POSTMODERN

Living with an architect, you either don't have the time or the money to do what you want for yourselves," says Birgitta Celsing by way of explanation for how her house, Klockberga, got to be the way it is. She and her late husband, prominent Swedish architect Peter Celsing, took over a property near the royal summer residence at Drottningholm in the late 1950s and gave it its present form some ten years later. Meaning to raze a solid but ordinary turn-of-the-century house to free the grassy hillside site for a plan of his own, Celsing found his intentions got side-stepped. After living with a make-do arrangement for nearly a decade, he opted to renovate the house, whose personality by then had encroached on his family's lives.

Perhaps the delay was fortuitous. What could have been a thoroughly modern landmark instead became a sketchbook of his ideas—with some of the themes reaching fruition in later projects. Celsing was a modernist who had not lost touch with the architectural past. While, some decades earlier, architect Gunnar Asplund had moved Sweden from the cool lines of the classical 1920s toward the clean forms of functionalism, Celsing deliberately resurrected selected motifs from antiquity to fuse his brand of modernism with a mannered timelessness.

In his own home, he experimented with various materials' tolerance of climatic demands, shaped sources of light to maximize their benefits, stretched classical axioms to fit the present, and readapted an existing structure to natural and manmade contexts. Klockberga is an old white sheep of a house in sleek, newer wolf's clothing, all the more cunning for how it foreshadowed postmod-

ern precepts. Celsing wrapped three sides of the exterior in black sheet metal—normally used as a roofing material—leaving the garden façade of white wood, and cut in oculus windows under peaks of the roof. Inside, he reshaped rooms and openings to admit east/west sunlight, illuminating the couple's very personal and humanistic style.

Klockberga hugs the grassy hill where the royal chapel bell is rung. Overscaled round windows make reference to court architecture. BOTTOM LEFT: *the living room's playful design ideas include a ceiling-hung tapestry, painted-sketch-paper walls, stenciled window treillage, drop-leaf radiator covers, a cascading rug over a sofa.* OPPOSITE: *the dining room,* TOP. *The entry hall's* faux fresco *ochre walls evoke the classical,* BOTTOM RIGHT; *a stripe of dark marble underfoot creates a support column's permanent "shadow." A round mirror over the door seems to pierce the space and alludes to oculus windows, as in the bedroom,* BOTTOM LEFT, *where a William Morris print covers the walls.*

OVERLEAF: *artist Olle Nyman helped choose colors for the front hall of the main structure and interior of the teahouse, shown here. All-over use of a strong Matisse blue gives an updated look to traditional Swedish hues. Classical exterior touches, picked out in white wood, tie it to the main house.*

DIGGING IN

When rain whips across the land in horizontal sheets, staying dry gets top priority. Building a house that stands up to these windswept, watery conditions presents its own problems—and, in Iceland, its own solutions. At about the turn of the century, concrete was discovered to have the bunkerlike properties needed to weather the island's unchecked winds and year-round precipitation. Imported timber became too costly to fuel twentieth-century building. In addition, the solid concrete took rather naturally to the functionalist houses of the 1930s and in postwar years has adapted to modern forms, frequently for the good, sometimes for the ill.

One residential architect who has proved her mettle in handling the massive material with grace is a woman called Hogna Sigurdardóttir. Not only does the home she planned for a family of seven serve their varied needs well, but it works with the surroundings in a way that pays tribute to the oldest Icelandic building traditions. The sod that is bermed against the house recalls the time-tested insulating properties of the first earth dwellings. Here, planted with grass and ground cover, the dense carpet of green embraces the sculptural shape of the house, uniting it with the landscape.

Artist Ragnheidur Jonsdóttir and her husband, Hafstein, charged Hogna, his cousin, with the design of an integrated space for them and their five sons that would work as a whole yet provide each member with room for retreat. She responded with a plan for a generous living area that includes kitchen/dining room and yards of seating space in a wraparound

banquette that encircles the other areas on three sides. Bedrooms, den, and Ragnheidur's atelier, a few steps up, form a second concentric circle around the main room. At the psychological and physical hub stands a handsome chimney column that warms the open room as it supports the structure.

In the living room, LEFT, a window wall and substantial glass pivot door open up the space to the outdoors between berms. Vigorous interior materials like flagstone and Norwegian fir hold up under the concrete's weight. Scoring the exterior concrete textures its surface with a harmonious grid, OPPOSITE. It is treated with silicone for water-resistance. Nicely rusted milk cans brimming with flowers sit on an outdoor patio, bordered by lava-stone retaining walls and shrubs.

The kitchen and dining areas, constructed of fir, form part of the whole. Up a level are pocket doors that slide back to reveal the boys' bedrooms; these spaces can be converted to other uses and remain open to the main area when the sons leave home. The dining table was used as a work surface both by printmaker Ragnheidur and by her children as students during their early years in the house. All table surfaces were varnished to protect them; now the stripped wood is simply oiled. RIGHT: a windowed bay brings daylight in; its emerald plantings enhance the interior. One of Ragnheidur's engravings hangs on an adjacent wall.

OVERLEAF: The load-bearing fireplace column was given sculptural prominence by the architect; skylights relieve its tension and funnel light into the center of the interior. Copper is used decoratively on the scored stack, inspiring a collection of metalware on built-in shelves below.

BALANCING ACT

Rejoicing on Midsummer night is an old pagan custom that has never outlived its merriment. It is the pre-Christian festive counterpart to Christmas; the nightless nights of June seem to be offered in divine balance to the murky days at year's end. While, in the absence of light, nature's palette recedes into wintry monochrome, in summer, high-saturation shades tease the eye at every turn. On the clearest days in the central province of Dalarna, a Swedish-blue sky makes a brilliant backdrop for intense leafy greens and the purple of distant hills. Yellows, blues, violets, pinks, and whites paint the fields in an irresistible bouquet of wildflower colors. Across the meadows, haymaking perfumes the air with a tangy sweetness. Nature tantalizes man to dance and sing her praises. She supplies both the cause and the means for the Midsummer celebration.

For the solstice weekend, people pack into trains, cars, buses, and boats to return to the soil, the forest, the water—to leave the confines of their towns and become recharged by the primitive pleasures of life outdoors. Birch branches adorn doorways, ship decks, and even truck grilles; chains of flowers are twined around flagstaffs, maypoles, and pale blond heads. In this, the most Swedish of Swedish provinces, it is a time to don traditional costumes, mischievously embrace cherished superstitions, parade through the village, and ride to church in a boat. A fiddler strikes up a folk tune at a dance by the lake. A young girl picks a bouquet of seven wildflowers to place under her pillow so that she will see her beloved in a dream. All generations forgo sleep, taste well-loved foods, make long toasts to the nightless night, spin round to the music—indulge until they lose their equilibrium in observance of nature's balance.

The flowery time of the summer solstice is celebrated with all-natural trimmings.
OPPOSITE: *the distinctive manner of drying hay in Dalarna makes a wall of functional art across mown fields.*

OVERLEAF: *a midsummer night's fiddler; a bedecked maypole in the late sunset.* PAGES 168–169: *the dining area of a one-room cabin, or stuga, now part of a larger house, is set up for Midsummer dinner. Local kurbits paintings, whose decorative storytelling motifs are distinctive for their use of fantasy flowers and play on scale, were found in the house.*

C H A P T E R   F O U R

I N   T O W N

The texture of life in the Scandinavian cities derives from the endurance of traditional lifestyles in the Nordic provinces. As late as 1939, seventy-five percent of the Finnish population was still rural, for example. While such figures have long since reversed themselves in all five countries, recent memory dictates that every Scandinavian is a country person at heart. The onset of the Industrial Revolution began to stimulate widespread migration to urban centers that had grown up as ports and trading centers on the coasts. With the exception of small northern mining towns that forced the development of communities for workers and company officials, outlying villages served mostly as legislative and religious meeting places and more or less retained their agrarian character. Simple single-story timber structures clustered in rows followed cobbled or dirt lanes. Indigenous stylistic uniformity gave unity to the whole; small scale kept the aspect human.

Most important to the character of the growing cities, the relative lateness of industrialization coincided with a rising tide of national spirit as these old cultures, though young modern nations, experienced the same romanticism that began to grip all of Europe in the wake of its disillusionment with the first sour fruits of the machine era. In a very real sense, Scandinavia profited by the Continent's mistakes. As art historian Kirk Varnedoe expresses it, "By lagging behind for much of the nineteenth century, Scandinavia thus found itself at the forefront of the European *fin de siècle* rejection of material progress. . . . As major economic collapses and the increasing polarization of social politics throughout Europe contributed to deepening pessimism over modernization and its attendant troubles, Northern lands and thought came to hold a special prestige, and less 'spoiled' Scandinavia gained a positive sense of its separateness." Progressive Scandinavians attempted to short-circuit the miseries wrought by factory-town life in Britain and elsewhere by subscribing to the philosophies of thinkers such as Englishmen John Ruskin and William Morris, who called for a return to nature and agrarian values in search of the good life. Groups of reformers gained a voice in Stockholm and Helsinki, spearheading the drive to guarantee quality living standards, including the right to light, clean air, and green recreational areas for those who were moving to cities to work in the new companies.

Near the beginning of the nineteenth century, a cool brand of classicism had left its imprint on the major Scandinavian capitals, giving a pale, elegant complexion to public buildings and an ordered pattern to the surrounding avenues of low structures. By the end of the century, English garden-town plans became inspirational models for new attached housing, and the British Arts and Crafts movement influenced the look of residential architecture and interiors. Apartment buildings were often simplified adaptations of Continental Jugendstil or more romantic, rusticated home-grown styles. Green pockets were planned to make everyday life more pleasant, and waterside areas were to be made accessible for both transportation and enjoyment. Social reformers suggested that aesthetics play an important role in the transitional period that was underway. "Swedish handicraft is the father of Swedish independence" was the slogan of the Society of Crafts and Design. The first such organization in the world, the Swedish Society was founded in 1945 to ensure that the legacy of the small artisan and country craftsman would be inherited by the furniture, glass, ceramic, and textile factories. Writer Ellen Key challenged the public in her booklet "Beauty for All" to create fine everyday objects for the common man. The Stockholm Exhibition of 1930 influenced all of Scandinavia with Swedish architect Gunnar Asplund's marvelous proposals for apartment living. And the designs of a young Finn called Alvar Aalto, also shown at the exhibition, foreshadowed the uniquely humanistic brand of functional modernism that was to distinguish his work and that of many of his Nordic colleagues.

Scandinavia's cities continued to develop, each at its own pace. Reykjavik in 1900 was a hamlet of just 6,000. Today, it retains traces of its agrarian past more than any of its sister capitals; Main Street, or Adalstraeti, follows the bridle path of the country's first settler in the late ninth century. Bergen originated in the twelfth century as a Hanseatic trading town; it still reveals the architectural influence of the German merchants. Oslo also felt the impact of Continental styles as Danish rule made its mark on building customs during critical periods of growth. Copenhagen likewise bears traces of early Dutch and German monumentality, but by the beginning of the twentieth century the Danes, too, were acknowledging that the precepts of international modernism responded to the clean lines and practicality of their native building styles in timber and then in brick, and could be modified to satisfy their new housing needs.

The 1960s initiated a period of enormous expansion all over Scandinavia, as elsewhere in the industrialized world, that resulted in scattered urban renewal and suburban growth, much of which has since met with criticism. Today, the keys to the future of good housing and design are being sought more often in the roots of early functionalism than in postmodern experimentation. At a landmark juncture, all across Scandinavia, the modern idiom was fused with the vernacular at the same time that it was adopted as a symbol of progress. It is an unusual marriage that has remained timely and goes far to explain why, in these countries, modern remains a popular expression and not just a design style.

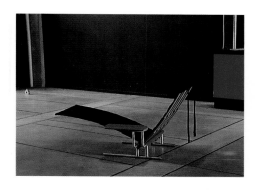

PRECEDING PAGES: *the steeply pitched rooftops of Bryggen, or the Wharf, in the west-coast Norwegian city of Bergen,* PAGE 171. *The structures were built in about 1300 on narrow lots that allowed city dwellers a maximum of water frontage. One of the crisp facades in the complex of painted-stucco neoclassical buildings in Helsinki's Senate Square,* PAGES 172–173, *all designed by noted architect Carl Ludwig Engel over a period of about twenty years, beginning in 1817. Engel, a German who had previously lived in St. Petersburg, was sent to the newly proclaimed capital of the Finnish grand duchy, in the period of tsarist rule, to fashion civic structures after Russian models.*

CLOCKWISE, FROM ABOVE: *a steel-and-wood chaise with canvas seat, designed by Erik Krogh for Altaform and introduced at Copenhagen's Scandinavian Furniture Fair in 1985. Stockholm children in colorful, warm clothing for outdoor winter play. Many houses in Reykjavik are covered in corrugated iron, a material used from the late nineteenth century to the present. Modern stucco garden apartments with fire ladder, required by law in Finland, interpreted along clean, contemporary lines. The harborside, open-air market in Helsinki gives a fresh country air to the capital city.*

PLAIN WHITE WRAPPER

When interior architect Kerstin Enbom found this two-room flat in one of Helsinki's beautifully preserved Jugendstil buildings, she grabbed it, knowing the generous proportions of the turn-of-the-century rooms would more than make up for there being only two of them. She turned the apartment into a working studio with enough amenities to make it also function agreeably as a *pied-à-terre*. Today, it has become a first apartment for her grown daughter.

Her decorating scheme brought clean ready-mades to a revamp of some of the built-in pieces and netted a maximum of workable space with a minimum cash outlay. A free hand with white fabric, furniture, and paint immediately gave life to the once-dark, woody interior. Heavy old doors were dip-stripped and left with that dry, attractive, nonyellow look that Scandinavian pine naturally acquires with age. Floors were varnished to high shine to contrast with old woodwork and the range of white furnishings. A sleeping loft was constructed over the kitchen area, suggesting a modern interpretation of the cozy pallets that were laid in the space atop massive stone ovens in some of the oldest Finnish log dwellings. Large windows, left unadorned, capitalize on daylight that shines through the apartment, bounced around by the all-white scheme. Inventive touches with stock items and unusual surfaces make the decorating difference.

Mirrored reveals and tile ledges update generously proportioned windows near the work table, LEFT. Space between a cabinet and loft-support post lends itself to built-in shelves adjacent to the bar-height kitchen table, BOTTOM LEFT. Red laminated panel inserts on kitchen cabinets were covered with adhesive paper; frames were painted white, OPPOSITE. A ladder leads to the sleeping loft overhead. The cut-to-size marble slab turns the plain pine cantilevered table into something special for dining or an ample work surface for baking. A second work table takes advantage of daylight at the far end of the room.

The beautiful glazed-tile stove, with familiar turn-of-the-century pine-bough motif, still heats the apartment, ABOVE. Placed next to it is a repainted Empire chair; each complements the other with differing scales and similar colors. Unbleached cotton covers made by Ms. Enbom tie together foam seating units. On the sleeping platform, RIGHT, two foam mattresses are wrapped in a bright Marimekko print by Fujiwo Ishimoto. The mirrored wall doubles the image of the serene, Japanese-like arrangement.

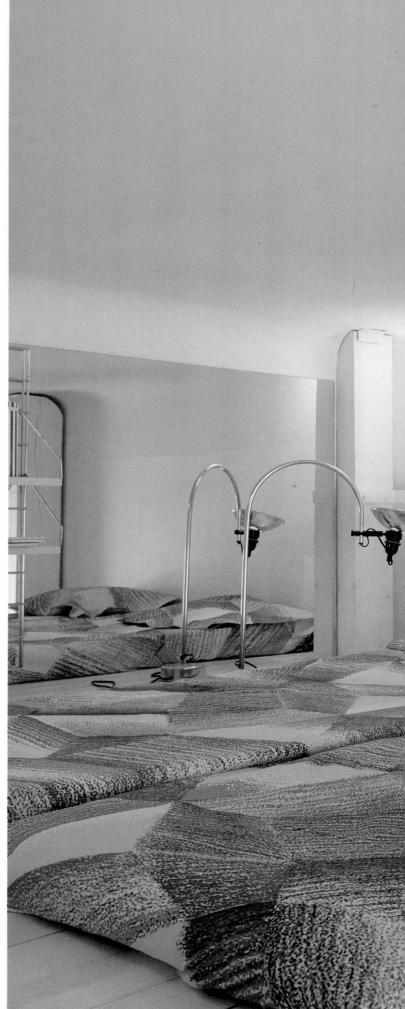

HISTORY'S HOLDOUT

A small wooden house seems unexceptional in the northern timberlands of Scandinavia. What sets this one apart is that it poses discreetly on a patch of green, indifferent to the Oslo traffic that whizzes by some yards down the hill. Before the king's castle was built close by and its park planned, a nineteenth-century poet, Henrik Wergeland, carved a modest parcel of land out of the countryside and had a home built big enough for himself and a couple of boarders upstairs. Proximity to royal property determined the unassuming dwelling's fate as the city grew up around it: in the 1920s it was purchased by the state, to be awarded for life to various artists of note. For the past six years, composer Arne Nordheim has made his home here with his wife, interior architect Rannveig Getz.

The simple regularity of the house's painted wood exterior does little to prepare a guest for the open feeling of the interior. Well proportioned, with generous window and door openings and trim, the rooms lend themselves not only to use as quiet creative spaces, but also as entertaining areas for friends in the arts or official parties. Ms. Getz's talent in juxtaposing furnishings from different eras and binding them with color makes a very personal home of a state residence. Her mix of old and new forms has purpose—to relate shapes and styles that have clear definition in order to highlight their likenesses while distinguishing them as well. Thus the unity of a Norwegian Empire settee, Italian arc lamp, round peasant's table, and Ms. Getz's grandmother's rocker is ensured by their rhyming curves. Adjacent walls are painted in a blue that stands up to

the certain lines. Three ample rooms open onto each other on the main floor, with a smaller music room for Mr. Nordheim off to one end. Upstairs, two bedrooms and a bath give onto a shared sitting loft, whose pitched walls follow the cottage's classic roof lines.

Forced tulips and birch leaves in a modern Norwegian glass vase herald the approach of spring, LEFT. *The house's front door,* BOTTOM LEFT. *A graceful nineteenth-century cast iron candelabrum tops a marble fireplace that has a beautiful Jugendstil hammered-copper surround,* OPPOSITE. *Reflected in the mirror is a contemporary iron chandelier by F. N. Bodvin.*

A living-room corner, OPPOSITE, combines an Afghan hanging, Danish sofas, Finnish vase by Alvar Aalto, and Norwegian wall cupboard with a curvaceous Ekstrem ("extreme") chair by modern designer Terje Ekstrøm. Light streaks across a central sitting room that adjoins Mr. Nordheim's studio and the house's big kitchen, ABOVE. A painted peasant cupboard relieves a black-and-white scheme of a Norwegian Empire dining set and classic teak chairs by Danish architect Finn Juhl. RIGHT: a detail of the chairs and a side table.

The large kitchen, ABOVE AND OPPOSITE, *forms the core space of the house. The seating area,* ABOVE, *is adjacent to the kitchen's cooking/dining space and is used informally. An ornate mirror, modern lighting, and nineteenth-century furniture from town and country mix in this welcoming setting. A detail from the sitting room,* LEFT, *shows a successful grouping of basic blacks.*

Shelves that span a kitchen window display a collection of Scandinavian glass, old and new, and cleverly camouflage a view of a modern office building across the street, ABOVE. An Alvar Aalto table and Mies van der Rohe chairs pull up to a chimney/counter configuration designed by Ms. Getz, RIGHT. Tables can be moved about to accommodate guests.

VIVID VISION

Planes of blue, white, charcoal, and sand in stucco and tile create exterior tension. A pergola walk is balanced by the verticality of a tower that marks the entry. A semicircular study that faces the rear garden, OPPOSITE, takes the edge off the structure's angularity.

The 1920s and 1930s were the delicious decades of early modern idea testing, the dawn of the era when Scandinavians made an indelible mark on the history of design with their own humanistic versions of functionalistic modernism. One visionary architect was Arne Korsmo, who believed that the goal of education is to teach people to see. His buildings in Oslo bear an international modern influence, gleaned in his travels to Europe and America to take in the manmade attractions of southern climes. Of his first major study tour to southern Europe in 1928 he wrote, "I was fascinated by all this history, but I kept wondering if it would be possible to smuggle the same joy into the logic of our time."

The home he completed for Axel Damman in Oslo in 1932 illustrates his success in infusing the functional with joy. He used color—especially the distinctive, dominant "Korsmo blue"—to call out a juxtaposition of vertical and horizontal volumes, creating a Constructivist whole. The house was innovative for its unity of the practical and ornamental. Garage, kitchen, and entrance all merge seamlessly into the geometric plan that squarely declares its modernity but sits as gently in natural surroundings as any older vernacular dwelling. Moreover, Korsmo's definition of an architect shows characteristic traces of naturalistic Scandinavian roots: "If he disturbs nature, he does so in order to make the whole into a larger synthesis."

Making It Real

trim and floors, Asklund produced a classical dwelling in today's terms. His manipulation of principles yields engaging results: the symmetry is thrown off a bit by unmatched side wings; the typically cool Nordic façade is supplanted by the banality of red brick; lighting fixtures are overscaled, making the "manor" appear mini; a formal gallery of double doors is painted a lowly farm-blue.

The house conveys an environmental message, too, without sacrificing its good looks. All-natural materials, from insulation to mortar-washed walls colored with a chalk-based pigment, allow it to breathe. Its main openings are oriented toward the south, with sitting and sleeping spaces there. And, structurally, it is as heavy as possible to enhance passive retention of heat.

In the master bedroom, which faces south, is a balanced collage of pieces from all periods, FAR LEFT. *Dining-room doors that open onto a limestone terrace form a series of "posts" with classically simple sconces,* LEFT. *The colors of the kitchen,* BOTTOM LEFT, *were planned with the help of artist Mariana Manner. On the north side the kitchen is buffered by pantry and wine cellar; glass cabinets facing south admit daylight and warmth.*

Architect Lars Asklund's interests run counter to the mainstream. He is an advocate of the authentic in an age of synthetic petroleum-derived products, a student of the classics force-fed the lessons of modernism, a disciple of the simple working in a complicated domain. Villa Ursing, a house he designed in the medieval city of Lund, in southern Sweden, is an attempt to resolve some of these contradictions.

Steeped in Danish and Swedish history, the surrounding province is proud of its estates, which grew wealthy on agriculture. Asklund's sense of fun led him to plan "a modern manor" in town for his clients, a couple whose grown children had moved out, leaving them free to re-create home-as-castle along purely adult lines. Using basic, genuine materials, like brick for walls, traditional tar paper for roofing, and wood for

The rear of the house has an off-center pediment, reflecting pool, and assymetric wings, with a bedroom in one wing and living room in the other, ABOVE. The red brick façade is punctuated with farmhouse-blue openings that are spaced to not quite line up. The entry hall's blue-washed paneling, RIGHT.

OVERLEAF: in the dining room, fine Gustavian chairs team up with a plain trestle table, antique metalwork, and the well-known lamp designed in 1958 by Danish designer Poul Henningsen.

SOURCE WORK

Looking out from the kitchen, FAR LEFT. The overmantle of wallboard, mirror, and acrylic tube, LEFT. OPPOSITE: smooth curly birch is done justice by the wraparound portico, TOP. Light walls and warm, natural wood set off a mixture of black modern classics by Jacobsen, Mies, and Le Corbusier, BOTTOM.

In countries where most modern archi-tects don't appear pressed to acquire the prefix "post-," Jan Digerud is some-thing of an individualist. Together with his partner, Jon Lundberg, he formed an archi-tectural firm whose name, Jan & Jon, is a clue to the serious commitment to a sense of play in its work. Like most adherents to the mixed-genre expression that is now responding to the parings-down of inter-national modern, the partners dip into the past for inspiration. When it comes to renovation, the firm opts for creating new forms within the existing interior frame to strengthen what exists by bringing some-thing different to it.

In his own newly acquired Oslo apart-ment, Mr. Digerud wants to bring out the bones of the Funkis (functionalist) building while injecting something of his interest in embellishment into the space. A kitchen opening that confronts the visitor directly on entering provided the occasion to create a grand inner portico that both acts sym-bolically and neatly camouflages the cooking area behind sliding doors. In addition, a playful/practical attitude toward the portico urged him to incorporate shelves, liquor cabinet, and dining surface into its design; its windowed opening admits daylight from the kitchen through to the hall. He brought out the unusual corner placement of a fire-place with an overmantle construction of solids, see-throughs, and mirrors. While the space is unfinished, it holds the promise of fulfilling a postmodernist's mixed-message hopes.

PERIOD PEACEFUL

The exterior of the joined houses, FAR LEFT, belies the variety of interior treatments. Enclosing an outdoor passage linked the structures and yielded a log-walled entry, LEFT. Cerulean blue and fresco red cast a modern chair and table by Swedish architect Bruno Mathsson in an unexpected light, BOTTOM LEFT. A small connecting hallway and its paintbox colors, OPPOSITE.

OVERLEAF: Diverse treatments of woodwork flavor the interior. A gilt-frame mirror offers smooth contrast to heavy log walls, TOP. A sitting room and library have glossy white tongue-and-groove ceiling and trim, eggshell-finish deck-gray floor and matte ochre paneled walls, BOTTOM. The handsome old timber ceiling gives character to the master bedroom, made in the former attic space, RIGHT.

There's not a right angle in the house," says Ulla Tarras-Wahlberg Bøe of the home that she shares with her husband, Alf, and son. They know all the angles, having themselves renovated the side-by-side structures nearly fifteen years ago. In what is now a designated landmark quarter in Oslo, a row of small timber houses present low-scale painted façades to a narrow street that climbs a hill, keeping secret their green yards that give onto a burbling river behind them. It is a scene that hints at the diminutive quality of town dwelling in the early nineteenth century (when one of the houses the Bøes now own was moved here from the country and the one next door was constructed) and at the civility of this sort of lifestyle in Norway's capital today.

The Bøes joined the two log houses by enclosing a narrow passage that led from the street to the rear yard, and they insulated the structures from the outside, enabling them to expose certain of the interior beams, log walls, and former attic's sloped ceiling. "Seiving out" the unwanteds from an accumulation of furniture, they decorated sparingly with a more-modern-than-old mix, resisting the urge to create a period piece within the romantic frame. A brave use of color further saves the rooms from nostalgic sweetness. Their design choices are informed but not overworked, fitting for an atmosphere intended to be both comfortable and peaceful enough to settle down in with a volume from one of the full walls of shelves.

HUMBLE FINDS, GRAND GESTURES

In a get-rich-quick effort, the 1898 building in which this apartment is located was thrown up in about six months. Local Oslo authorities found it too bulky for the neighborhood and ordered it torn down, but the owners successfully appealed the decision by promising to take the extraordinary measure of ornamenting the façade with Pompeii-inspired frescoes. Sadly, these now lie buried under a nasty coat of yellow paint that was applied in the 1930s.

Moved by its painterly past and the impressive scale of the rooms in a large apartment that was built to sell quickly and fetch a high price, architect and writer Tomas Thiis-Evansen and his art-instructor wife fell into the spirit of decorating it with grand gestures. They positioned mirrors at either end of the space's main axis—in the parlor and behind the bed—to strengthen its plan, and they observed a policy of fill-but-don't-overstuff in their approach to decorating the rooms, using some family hand-me-downs and many secondhand finds. Believing in the virtues of handcrafting, in the best Scandinavian domestic tradition, Mr. Thiis-Evansen and his family of five set about refinishing these pieces. The "pseudo-Rococo" carved-plaster parlor mirror is of a type that was cranked out in large numbers at the turn of the century. The couple's bed is made from an old organ, a castoff from a church undergoing restoration.

In winter, the usable space shrinks by half when the Thiis-Evansens close off the airier front rooms, decorated in light colors, and retreat to the inner living/dining room with its inviting tile stove and spacious kitchen with massive hearth.

The innermost rooms—kitchen, ABOVE, and living/dining room—are painted deep blue. In one of the sunny parlors, OPPOSITE, a mirror marks the main axis; classical columns, designed by the owner, connect it with the adjoining room.

OVERLEAF: a "family portrait" in ceramic by Mrs. Thiis-Evansen hangs by the tile stove in the living/dining room, LEFT. The bed, formerly a church organ, creates a comfortable sleeping space within the very large bedroom, RIGHT.

Please Touch

Each narrow row house (the Guttmanns' is the red one, FAR LEFT) has a long lot that makes up in garden space for its somewhat cramped interior. Nets on an outbuilding recall the original occupants, LEFT. Wonderfully weathered outdoor furniture, two teahouses, and bits of old sculpture sit as usable "ruins" amidst tendrils and branches, ABOVE AND OPPOSITE.

No precious display of priceless treasures this—Max Guttmann's home may be a collector's paradise, but it's quite happily a hands-on habitat. Twenty-five years ago, Mr. Guttmann, a student of local history and antique home objects, made his first investment, one that has since shaped his professional and private worlds. A row of old fishermen's houses seemed slated for demolition as the Danish city of Elsinore developed plans to build a park on the site. For the equivalent of less than $2,000 he bought one of the houses, dating from the seventeenth-century, with the intention of studying it before it was razed. After five years, the line of little houses was saved, and Max gained permanent title to an invaluable property that he painstakingly began to turn into a home.

Many of the first furnishings, like the house, were regarded as throwaways when Mr. Guttmann, now an antiques dealer, scooped them up. Today, the interior is all of a piece, with the more pricey items tucked in amongst the others. Nothing is off-limits to the family of four. Slightly tattered hems take the edge off an old textile's dignity. Already scarred surfaces encourage Max's daughters to chop vegetables on a vintage kitchen cabinet. And his wife, Birgitta, with all the deftness of a set designer, seamlessly incorporates each new find into the whole and runs her home like any modern one.

In a den hang nineteenth-century animal paintings purchased intact in panels, ABOVE. The secretary, LEFT, sits near the front door, whose original marbleizing was discovered intact under twenty years of paint.

In the living room, burgundy paint was revealed when twentieth-century wallpaper and paint were stripped away, ABOVE. Blues in an eighteenth-century chandelier, painted farm cabinet, and porcelains contrast with deep-toned furnishings. A faux wood nineteenth-century chest, RIGHT, was Mr. Guttmann's first purchase, spied in a farm's attic when the thatch of the roof was removed for repair.

The stove found in the house still works, supplemented by an electric cooktop, ABOVE. Bits of pottery and a hen collection roost above an old pharmacist's cabinet that now houses the kitchen sink, RIGHT.

OVERLEAF: The dining area's spindle-back chairs, crocheted curtains, and window-sill collections are silhouetted in the sun from the street side of the house.

Changing Attractions Now Showing

A sewing factory that has been turned into a living loft is no longer an unusual alteration. This one in Reykjavik is testimony to similar conversions in some Scandinavian cities.

On a main shopping street in Iceland's capital, an old upstairs factory space was first reused by a group of filmmakers. Then two of the group seized on the chance to take over the loft when the company moved on. Today, Karl Oskarsson and Jon Tryggasson run their own firm, Frost Films, and share the loft for relaxed living after their long days of shooting. An irreverent intermingling of things at hand, castoffs, and friends' concoctions form a living collage that absorbs any number of people with little bother and no fuss. An old candy counter, a grand piano, a ballroom chandelier, pine dining set, and modular seating—casual acquaintances at first—became committed, lasting friends when Mr. Oskarsson and Mr. Tryggasson arranged them. A few graphics, old cottons, and a stuffed owl or two happened to fill in the holes, while a parachute, apparently dropped at random, seemed to make the seating float pleasingly on a calm gray sea of deck paint. And so it will stay until someone offers up another special outcast, or a prop is discovered that asks to come home.

The candy counter, ABOVE, *is used to separate the main room from the kitchen. A parachute throw makes an appealing muddle of standard modular seating,* OPPOSITE TOP. *Textiles are swagged from the ceiling with string, shirred on an old screen, or worked into a piece of art,* OPPOSITE AND OVERLEAF. *Frames lean here and there, some with prints, some without.*

C H A P T E R   F I V E

GREAT ESCAPES

If the harshness of winter draws Scandinavians together, the exuberance of summer scatters them into the farthest reaches of the countryside. Long, light days when the sun never sets pull people outdoors and away from the cities where contemporary life has resettled them, and even deeper into the hinterlands for those who live in outlying villages. Even in southern areas, where the sun sinks below the horizon sometime before midnight, perpetual twilight can bridge the night hours in the high latitudes at this time of the year. As Finnish author Zachris Topelius wrote of his countryman, "Midwinter darkness has taught him to love the light."

Nature breaks her winter silence and speaks again with great animation. The senses are reawakened by the fragile, chartreuse light cast by the first tender leaves in beech or birch forests, by the fresh bite of the season's first dill, by the song of the nightingale back from its North African migration, by the pungency of cut grass at haymaking time, by the lingering sharp scent from a small wood smokehouse near the water's edge after the afternoon's catch of fish is retrieved.

Winter's industriousness is offset by summer's play. Businesses close early, lengthening after-work boating hours to the full equivalent of a Saturday's sail in other climates. Anyone might put aside his labors on an especially delicious afternoon and spend it outside—with full moral impunity. There is unanimous assent among serious, winter-pale Scandinavians regarding everyone's right to take off when nature beckons. A weekend cottage is no more a luxury than the family car. Its use is assured on month-long vacations, weekends, and particularly lovely evenings, if it lies close enough to make weeknight visits practical. Children are shuttled off to the country at the end of the school year; the fall term must tame them again after two months of running barefoot through fields and splashing naked in the sea.

In summer houses, as in many things Scandinavian, simple is best. Tiny dwellings are tucked in narrow Norwegian valleys between fjord and mountain, where summer temperatures can reach ninety degrees and orchards bloom with fruit and nut trees. Cottages are dotted about in the huge archipelago of islands that lie like natural stepping stones between the southern coasts of Sweden and Finland. Lakeside cabins in the northern forests restore the cherished solitude relinquished in exchange for the convenience of city life. Modest beach houses squat behind rose hedges in one-shop villages, a dirt lane away from the shore. Even in places where permanent structures aren't feasible, tents are pitched for summer's simple pleasures. Iceland's interior wilderness calls to those adventurous enough to ford its unbridged glacial streams, clean enough to drink from; thermal spring-fed outdoor pools act as natural hot tubs on fifty-degree July days.

Grand seventeenth- and eighteenth-century homes often had outdoor wooden pavilions designed in a style befitting the house, the nicest with hand-painted murals making light of canvas-covered walls. Here, people took tea in the garden or ate supper in the warmth of the late-setting sun. The largest of these could serve for sleeping, too—an airy change of locale from much-used hearth and home. But even summer in more modest homes could involve a shift of scene. In northerly dairy districts, cows, goats, and sheep were pastured in the highlands in the warmer months, and a group of hands was sent along to tend them and live in rustic structures there. In timber homesteads, family members moved to unheated outbuildings—the lofts above grain barns, or clothing storehouses whose interiors could be decorated with farm textiles hung for the season to add lightness to deep-toned log walls.

By the mid-nineteenth century, well-to-do merchants began to take their families to the country for a healthy change of air from the growing towns. At first they boarded with rural families, who themselves moved into outbuildings; later they built their own homes as finances allowed. Artists went to the coasts of Denmark, Norway, and Finland and to the forests of central Sweden and Finland for clear air and light, and to seek valid subject matter among unspoiled country folk. Before World War II, the idea of a green plot of one's own had become so popular that city governments started programs to let small garden lots, each with a simple wood hut—now commonly known as garden colonies—to those who couldn't afford to escape to the countryside.

The past's rustic building styles are particularly well-suited to today's cabin in the woods, from squared-log structures to painted wood shapes. Solutions tend toward modern adaptations of yesterday's techniques, rather than reproduction looks. Farmhouses, barns, fishermen's huts, and miner's cottages, abandoned during migrations that accompanied economic downturns and industrial development, have been renovated for weekend use or sometimes moved to more suitable locales. Since the late nineteenth century, summer-house designs have offered a testing ground for architects, permitting them freer experimentation than the climatic demands of year-round living allow. But no matter what the quarters, primitive is often the preferred way of summer living, with outdoor bathing and a hand pump for water, a central chimney for cooking and heating, sometimes no power other than that generated by people—in a deliberate attempt to recapture the primal spirit of survival in northern lands.

PRECEDING PAGES: *a summer cabin, reachable only by boat, on a slope of Norway's remote Aurlandsfjord,* PAGE 215. *Sailboats on the Danish horizon,* PAGES 216–217.

CLOCKWISE, FROM ABOVE: *deck chairs facing the Baltic Sea. The village of Brekkestø on the south coast of Norway; the cottages— many now vacation homes—were originally painted white so they could be seen from the sea by their fisherman-owners. Raffia-tied garden bouquets readied as a summer hostess gift. A summerhouse garden with homemade painted furniture. Sign of comfort on a small Finnish island in the archipelago, where it is possible to reserve one of the few berths for an overnight stay.*

COVERING ALL THE ANGLES

A little prism of a house clad in green-painted wood has silvered in the sea breeze since it was built in the 1970s on commission by architect Jan Gezelius. In a village of mostly nineteenth-century vacation houses south of Stockholm, it stands out for its odd form and unusual placement. Wedged between a boulder and the yard of an older house, the two-story shape lifts its owners above obstacles to give them a crow's-nest view of the sea and white sails.

Gezelius, whose design for Stockholm's Ethnographic Museum is well known, applied a similar kind of architectural alchemy here. For each structure, he transformed familiar board and batten—in reference to the Swedish vernacular style—into an exotic shape with sophisticated lines. Here, a house without parallel walls makes interesting living spaces of a cluster of first-floor rooms topped off with a library/den, whose high ceiling and gabled window give it a more spacious appearance. Corner cutouts draw nature inside and bring sparkle to the rooms. The architect conceived the spunky plan after a trip to the United States, where the shapes of water towers caught his eye. Enjoyment of the offbeat has clearly captivated the hearts of its owners, who have brought to the house an idiosyncratic assortment of furnishings that just suit their warm-weather needs.

LEFT: *a sheltered spot of turf near the sea furnishes just enough footage for the small tower house with its cutout windows.* OPPOSITE, CLOCKWISE: *the granite boulder provides privacy for outdoor showers. A dining area just fits an alcove with one gently rounded wall. The upstairs room and its amusing amalgam—eighteenth-century gate-leg table, Hungarian candelabrum, comfortable wicker, a touch of Marimekko fabric. The turned stairs and their windowed dead-end finish.*

SMALL PLEASURES

It was a happy and important period in my life," says Norwegian architect Per-Johan Eriksen, "and this was a fantastic way to work with a house." Some twenty years ago, when his practice was young, Mr. Eriksen set off with sketches to the rocky site on the south coast of Norway and began to build a summer cottage for himself and his wife. "A house is like clothing," he adds. "You want to be comfortable in it." A tall young man fueled by energetic idealism, he worked with the specs of his plans, the idiosyncratic shapes of the rocks, and what felt good in relation to his own lanky dimensions to strike a balance he hoped would honor the landscape as well as the users. He was inspired by Frank Lloyd Wright, who had similarly site-built a house at Taliesin.

Structuring the house taught Mr. Eriksen architectural simplicity, a lesson that suits the summer philosophy of most Scandinavians. By the time warm weather turns them outside, their indoor pleasures have all been sated. A summer house must not stand in the way of their relishing the season outdoors. Shelter, somewhere to sleep, and a place to cook are all the Eriksens wanted of a weekend place. The cottage he built satisfied these needs with only a few rooms: two small bedrooms joined to the living/dining area by a corridor kitchen that shares a large stuccoed brick hearth with the open area. The wooden cabin was painted black to disappear into the rocks. A freestanding atelier/guesthouse was built three years ago and linked to the cottage by a wooden deck that affords privacy and acts as a fair-weather room.

The dark-stained house sits on the rocky coast, its windows mirroring the bluest sky and sea, BELOW. *The well-planned all-wood interior attends to all needs without show or fuss,* OPPOSITE.

INNOCENCE REGAINED

This neoclassical-style thatched cottage is infamous in the sleepy village on the coast of North Zealand, where it was built in 1918. It is known not only for being the first charmer in a neighborhood of vacation houses neatly sequestered behind hedges and apple trees, but for its grisly role as a kind of corpse depot for the Nazis during their occupation of Denmark. Local workers refuse to stay alone in the house they call "the Chapel." After World War II, the house stood vacant for years, open to the winds and rain that blow in from the sea.

Things looked rosier in the 1950s, when the then-pink pavilion was bought by a painter who tended its wounds. Architect-trained designer Ole Kortzau took it over in 1981 after eyeing it for years from a less notorious weekend home nearby. He repainted the outside, using the traditional mix of lime and iron dust seen so often in Scandinavia; it will darken naturally with the passage of time. White wainscoted walls give the rooms an airy, summery look. Furnishings from different periods are mostly painted, too, for the sort of summer-white style that pulls all the charming odd bits together.

The exterior of the 900-square-foot thatched cottage, a romantic octagon with balcony and shuttered French doors, ABOVE LEFT. *The bedroom's vaulted window reveal gives onto the balcony,* ABOVE; *nearby are one of Mr. Kortzau's prints and a rug of his design.* OPPOSITE: *summer house trappings, including one of Mr. Kortzau's beach-bag designs.*

Looking into the living room, OPPOSITE. Inside, a bench-sized niche just fits under a turned staircase picked out in gray, ABOVE. A pair of slab-side sofas from the 1930s are upholstered in a linen print by architect Josef Frank, an Austrian who lived and worked in Sweden from 1934 until his death in 1967, RIGHT.

ALL IN A SUMMER'S WORK

Spurts of building over the course of about thirty years account for the charmingly choppy shape of a fisherman's-cottage-turned-summer-house on the Baltic Sea east of Helsinki. This method not only allowed the house to become big enough to handle the five-member Enbom family, but it also enabled the project-oriented owner to content himself with productive work during each summer stay. The three-room shelter, poised at the edge of granite cliffs, took a first turn with Sten Enbom's addition of a covered porch and third bedroom; it grew again when a sun porch extended the living room out under the birches. Sauna and piers were added down by the sea, gazebo and playhouse cropped up atop mossy boulders above; everything was owner-constructed.

Living on different levels nestled between rocks facilitates shifts of scene for entertaining and play. Gangways that encircle the small cove berth a couple of boats and make the water accessible for swimming. They are sometimes set up to accommodate crayfish parties, offering a breezy change from the two dining areas on the upper decks.

The interior changes with each season, too, incorporating refinished finds and new wallpaper and paint. Kerstin Enbom, an interior architect, comes to stay for the summer with the children, bringing along the odd piece she has purchased in the interim plus plans for redecorating another area. With all the small comforts added over time, it is significant that the owners choose to disturb the original flavor of the house as little as possible. Electricity was eventually brought in to aid in cooking, but water is still pumped by hand, and sauna and outhouse are used instead of a bathroom.

LEFT: *the cottage's white-trimmed exterior is seen through rowans and birches from the upper cliffs. Like much of the house, the docks and gazebo are owner-built.* OPPOSITE: *sponge-painted washstand, wallpaper-framed mirror, and stripped nineteenth-century chair make a cheery bathing area in a bedroom corner.*

The hearth and built-in woodbox are of Mr. Enbom's design, OPPOSITE; the stark farm furniture and modern pendant lamp are tempered with fresh flowers, and with bouquets of home-grown flowers strung up to dry, ABOVE. A china cabinet is trimmed with paper lace and decals, RIGHT.

WOODSMAN'S HOLIDAY

We asked for a wood house with a wood floor and we got a masonry house with a masonry floor," says Dorrit Petersen of the weekend home planned for her family by architect Gehrdt Bornebusch. Poul Petersen, a forestry administrator, had chosen the site near the Danish coast as one that would seclude himself and his family happily in their favorite surroundings, the woods. But to their ultimate delight, the architect was less obvious in his choice of a material that would strike its own sort of kinship with the forest. The simple slice of a house, interpreted in crusty mortar-washed brick, sits like a primeval shelter discovered in a clearing, perhaps a section of old rampart to which nature is laying claim with bits of moss and climbing vines. It is at once old and new, a timeless form in primary materials whose unbroken lines and crude surface evoke the paradoxical feelings of recognition and surprise that art can trigger.

The house's slight crescent-moon curve reinforces its situation at the edge of the forest, and opens it toward the light while closing it toward the trees. A pine-needled path leads up to the two semicircular forms that project out midway along the protective convex northern wall, with its few openings primitively covered by clamped-on panes. The house's reclusiveness urges exploration. Through the unassuming entry, in one of the projections, lies an undivided interior; large windows disclose the grassy clearing on the other side of the house. A continuous floor of heavy brick makes a single surface of the living space, hearth, and terrace. Largely built-in furnishings grow out of the masonry envelope, accenting its appealing roughness with the evenness of tile or wood. The peeled-log ceiling speaks quietly of the environment and follows the lean-to slant of the wood-slat roof. Transverse brick walls near each end of the room conceal sleeping spaces and stop short of the ceiling to emphasize the form's curve.

The few small windows that pierce the north façade twinkle like gemstones when lit at twilight, ABOVE LEFT. *A long banquette follows the house's gentle curve in the main seating area,* ABOVE CENTER. *Glass that butts directly with brick brings light and green views to pocket-sized bedrooms,* ABOVE. *The fireplace's sensuous curve gives substance to the otherwise transparent south side of the house,* OPPOSITE. *Dining area and kitchen are one with the living space.*

OVERLEAF: *facing a clearing, the south façade glows in the waning daylight. A weathered shed-type roof and crusty brick exterior humble the well-thought-out structure.*

FINDING THE PRECIOUS IN THE PLAIN

Anxious to speak the simple language of art without pretension, architect Knut Knutsen may have mastered the tongue at its elegant and elementary best in the summer house he built for himself in 1949 on the south coast of Norway. Sitting with his carpenters and masons in the rocky landscape a hundred yards from the surf, he instructed them to shape a shelter that would blend into the gray granite surroundings like a chameleon. The wood bungalow, whose undulating roof artfully mimics the roll of the coastal shelf, all but rests against a rock ledge along one full side and hides in the shade of pines and shore scrub on the other. Pine needles pile up in the slats of the wooden roof, trim paint grays with each season, loose rocks with twigs and pine cones as natural "mortar" find a permanent place as stepping stones up to a double door. Nearly forty years after it was completed, there is still no path to the house from the narrow lane nearby that dead-ends at the sea. Only a few well-trained eyes find the occasional piles of loose stones that identify the easiest up-and-down route in to the place. Suddenly, the dark roof becomes visible in the distance, only to disappear again as one turns to step across a brook and maneuver the next climb. If privacy was one concern in locating the house, even more of

a challenge was placing it in nature so as to leave the coast undisturbed.

The accident of birth fixed Knutsen in a spot on the architectural spectrum between the Arts and Crafts-inspired Nordic romanticism that flourished at the beginning of the twentieth century and the functionalism of the modern movement that swept surfaces clean starting in the 1930s. This house shows traces of both. Cottage-style clapboard covers two main sections: a family room with sitting/dining areas and small kitchen; and a wing of sleeping spaces and washroom, whose simple linearity seems to borrow from a bunkhouse plan. Mullioned windows, plank floor, and paneled ceiling carry the cottage aura inside. So do the checkered cottons and striped rag rugs that layer the interior with likably fading pattern. But continuity of material, iconic use of natural coloration within a black-and-white envelope, and the informed informality of interiors assign a cleaned-up, modern aspect to the whole. Like Alvar Aalto in Finland, Knutsen was a modernist with romance in his heart. While these influences put his work in a historical context, the deliberate simplicity of his expression gives it the timelessness of everyman's art.

The all-wood exterior of the summer house is painted black on the approach sides so that it falls into the shadow of the rock and pines, ABOVE LEFT. *The bedroom wing that turns in toward the main section is given the lift of white, perhaps in deference to its facing the morning light,* RIGHT. OPPOSITE: *the family washroom with its pickled-pine and blue-painted planes,* TOP; *a bowl of field flowers on the covered porch that connects the bedrooms and main section,* BOTTOM.

The intentional simplicity of the interiors bridges the influence of cottage and modern styles. The main section's dining area with Picassoesque family-made paper plates, RIGHT; one of the invitingly Spartan bedrooms, ABOVE.

ISLAND IDYLL

On a family-owned island off the coast of Finland, this little red cottage is one of many such discreet beacons for owners who come by boat to find safe harbor from the squalls of city life. In the customary way, the several cabins on the island are put to different uses; a wood-burning sauna is for bathing; a couple of structures are sleeping huts; others are for storage of equipment and food. True to historical spirit, few modern conveniences have intruded into the setting, so oil lamps or candles light the rooms and guests rely on "outdoor plumbing." In the only major alteration, architect Bertel Gripenberg had fold-away glass doors installed across the front of the main cottage, opening its living room fully to the porch and the outdoors.

Formerly a fisherman's home, the island saw use, like many of the thousands that fringe the Finnish shore, as a fishing base and for grazing. In warm weather, sheep were brought to feed in the meadows of this and neighboring islands.

A Quiet Cabin

The small barns, or *aittas*, of Finland are noticeably plainer than their decoratively carved counterparts in Norway. That strictness of line is representative of most Finnish architecture and design, whether historic or modern, and makes for an easy marriage of line for objects from most periods. Further, rustic design, whether old or reproduction, is spared the geegaws and curlicues that can detract from its primitive beauty.

The squared logs of this barn, with its overhung balcony and simple white windows, give it a clean appearance that has not been marred by interior renovation. Left exposed inside, and stain-treated for weather outside, the six-inch-thick members need no further insulation. Fittings were chosen to complement the strong lines of the structure and the self-sufficient requirements of its location on the offshore island. A new central hearth that services both living and cooking areas was installed, its bricks painted white for contrast with the deep wood texture of the walls. Odd-lot pieces include a barrel chair made from a birch stump, one of those marvelously inventive by-products of wartime scarcity—known as trench art in Finland. A new pine table, old trundle bed, and Jugendstil painted chairs all calmly combine in the two main rooms. Candles and oil lamps glow in the dimness, casting deeper shadows against quiet, dark log walls.

A white glider from the 1940s adds an unexpected "lacy" touch on the porch of the barn, ABOVE; *two sleeping lofts are reached by the outdoor ladders,* TOP. *The all-of-a-piece birch chair sits near a cupboard and copper implements by the front door,* OPPOSITE.

A jug of water magnifies candlelight from behind it, ABOVE. The chair is a Finnish adaptation of the Boston rocker, popular in the nineteenth century. Hearth and timbered half-wall define the two rooms of the living space, LEFT. A long farmhouse table is fronted by Jugendstil chairs whose green-blue finish harmonizes with old glass, OPPOSITE.

FLOWER FANCIES

An early twentieth-century idea—to rent out small plots of land on which to grow flowers and vegetables to town dwellers who could not afford their own places in the country—ultimately blossomed into exuberant garden-with-cottage colonies that hug the outskirts of some of the major Scandinavian cities.

Renters' imaginations seemed to be fired by ways to personalize the small sheds, so plain huts grew into tiny but distinctive shelters for weekending in the blossoms. Here, one such allotment garden on the fringes of Helsinki, with its whimsical houses, hedges, gates, and walks, is nourished as much with color and creativity as with water and soil.

Selected Bibliography

af Segerstad, Ulf Hård. *Carl Larsson's Home.* Reading, Massachusetts: Addison-Wesley, 1978.

Ágústsson, Hödur. *Building Through the Centuries.* Reykjavik, 1986.

Ailonen, Riitta, and Ritva Kinnunen. *Seurasaari Open-Air Museum.* Helsinki: National Board of Antiquities and Historical Movements, 1980.

Annandale, Nelson. *The Faroes and Iceland: Studies in Island Life.* New York: AMS Press, 1905.

Bjornstad, Arne, Per-Olof Palm, and Christina Westberg, eds. *Skansen.* Stockholm (n.d.).

Bowman, Monica, ed. *Design in Sweden.* Stockholm: The Swedish Institute, 1985.

Brace, Charles L. *The Norse Folk.* New York: Scribners, 1857.

Brooklyn Museum, The. *Carl Larsson.* New York: Holt, Rinehart and Winston, 1983.

Campbell, Olive Dame. *The Danish Folk School: Its Influence in the Life of Denmark and the North.* New York: Macmillan, 1928.

Clutterbuck, W. J., and J. A. Lees. *Three in Norway by Two of Them.* Oslo: Forlaget Tanum-Norli, 1882 and 1984.

Derry, T. K. *A History of Scandinavia.* Minneapolis: University of Minnesota Press, 1979.

Faber, Tobias. *New Danish Architecture.* Stuttgart: Verlag Gerd Hatje, 1968.

Franck, Harry Alverson. *A Scandinavian Summer.* New York: The Century Company, 1930.

"How the Danes Live." Special issue of the *Danish Journal.* Copenhagen: Royal Danish Ministry of Foreign Affairs, 1981.

Hultin, Olof, ed. *Architecture in Sweden: 1973–1983.* Stockholm: Arkitektur Forlag AB, 1983.

Lundahl, Gunilla, ed. *Recent Developments in Swedish Architecture, A Reappraisal.* Uppsala, Sweden: The Swedish Institute, 1983.

Martin, Anthony. *Norwegian Life and Landscape.* London: ELEK Books, 1952.

Mikkola, Kirmo. *Architecture in Finland in the 20th Century.* Helsinki: Finnish American Cultural Institute, 1981.

National Museum of Finland. Helsinki: National Board of Antiquities and Historical Monuments, 1980.

Nordic Enigma, The. Daedalus, vol. 113, no. 1. Journal of the American Academy of Arts and Sciences. Cambridge, Massachusetts: 1984.

Nordic Voices. Daedalus, vol. 113, no. 2. Journal of the American Academy of Arts and Sciences. Cambridge, Massachusetts: 1984.

Protection of the Architectural Heritage of Sweden. Stockholm: Central Office of Antiquities, 1975.

Redlich, Monica. *Denmark, Places and People.* Copenhagen: Schoenberg, 1948.

Sanders, Pamela. *Iceland.* Salem, New Hampshire: Salem House, 1985.

Smith, G. E. Kidder. *Sweden Builds.* New York: Reinhold, 1957.

Somme, Axel, ed. *The Geography of Norden.* New York: John Wiley & Sons, 1961.

Tvedten, Arne Sigmund, and Bengt Espen Knutsen. *Knut Knutsen.* Oslo: Gyldendal Norsk Forlag, 1982.

Varnedoe, Kirk. *Northern Light.* New York: Brooklyn Museum, 1982.

von Heidenstrom, Oscar Gustaf. *Swedish Life in Town and Country.* New York: G. P. Putnam's Sons, 1904.

INDEX

ACKNOWLEDGMENTS

The author wishes to give special thanks to Hördur Ágústsson, Walter Anderson, Gayle Benderoff, Gudmundur Benediktsson, Ulla Tarras-Wahlberg Bøe, Monica Boman, Pamela and Marshall Brement, David Breul, Roy Finamore, Deborah Geltman, Ranveig Getz, Arto Hallokorpi, Valdimar Hardarson, Jan Henriksson, Ron Hillary, Olaf Hultin, Tove Kjaer, Ilmari Kostiainen, Patricia McFate, Marín Magnusdóttir, Jukka Mantynen, Arne Nordheim, Steen Estvad Petersen, Christel Rosenlew, Ult Hård af Segerstad, Elizabeth Seip, Maitsu Sihvonen, Celia Woodley. To the American Scandinavian Foundation, the Societies of Crafts and Design and Tourist Offices of Denmark, Finland, Iceland, Norway, and Sweden, to Icelandair and Scandinavian Airlines for transportation, and to all those who opened their doors.

Design: Paul Zakris
Composed in Perpetua by Trufont Typographers, Inc., Hicksville, New York
Printed and bound by Toppan Printing Company, Ltd., Tokyo, Japan